Bible biographies
Series editor: David Jackman

Elijah

I dedicate this book to:
the community at Stella Carmel who were God's angels to wake me and feed me while I followed Elijah's footsteps (1 Kings 19:5–7); and members of St Helen's, Bishopsgate's 'Really Arty Weekend', 1988, who took this ancient story and brought it memorably back to life (1 Kings 17:22–23).

Elijah
Standing for God in a hostile world

Lance Pierson

Inter-Varsity Press

INTER-VARSITY PRESS
38 De Montfort Street, Leicester LE1 7GP, England

Unless otherwise stated, quotations from the Bible are from Good News Bible (Today's English Version) published by the Bible Societies and Collins, © American Bible Society, New York, 1966, 1971, 1976.

First published 1989

British Library Cataloguing in Publication Data

Pierson, Lance
  Elijah.
  1. Bible. O.T. Elijah
  I. Title II. Series
  222'50924

ISBN 0–85110–839–3

Set in 11/12 Linotron Times

Typeset in Great Britain by
Input Typesetting Ltd, London
Printed in Great Britain by
Cox & Wyman Ltd, Reading

Inter-Varsity Press is the book-publishing division of the Universities and Colleges Christian Fellowship (formerly the Inter-Varsity Fellowship), a student movement linking Christian Unions in universities and colleges throughout the United Kingdom and the Republic of Ireland, and a member movement of the International Fellowship of Evangelical Students. For information about local and national activities write to UCCF, 38 De Montfort Street, Leicester LE1 7GP.

Contents

General preface

For many Christians today the Old Testament is almost a closed book. There is comparatively little preaching of it from our pulpits, and even less personal study (apart from a few well-loved and well-worn purple passages). In an age when even the familiar stories of the ministry of Jesus, as recorded in the New Testament gospels, are increasingly unknown among children and young people generally, it is not surprising that many of these same people hardly know where to begin when they come to know Christ personally and are told to read the whole Bible.

This series is an attempt to meet that need, at a level that young Christians can readily understand and in a way with which they will be able easily to identify. It seeks to present an attractive way in, particularly to the Old Testament and its riches, because it starts where we all are – with the everyday life experience of real people. By mining the rich veins of biography and true story, we hope to set the Bible characters in their own time and background, allowing them to speak with their own authentic voice. This will be true to their own experience of God and so always faithful in opening up the biblical text. But at the same time the series seeks to bring the characters out of the pages of biblical history into our own very different culture. In doing so, the unchanging truths their stories expound and illustrate are applied to the practical business of living for God in the world of the late twentieth century.

Each contributor has been given considerable freedom in their style and treatment of their subject. This is because the range of biblical material is wide and varied, and also it illustrates that opening up and applying the Bible's message does not need to be confined to one style or stereotype. Some writers will be more closely tied to the biblical text than others; but all are united in their common belief in its authority, and therefore its unrivalled relevance. And all are united in their conviction that as we let the Bible speak for our present generation, as for all its predecessors, we shall hear the Word of the Lord, which lasts for ever. This is the prayer with which these books are sent out. I hope you will be able to echo it, and to experience its answer.

D. J. Jackman
Above Bar Church
Southampton

Acknowledgments

I have had a soft spot for Elijah ever since I 'discovered' 1 Kings 17 during the English summer of drought in 1976, and 1 Kings 19 during a long spell of depression the following year.

Many preachers and writers have helped me understand better the Bible chapters about him; I have tried to list them in the 'For further study' section at the end of the book. I particularly want to give thanks here to David Pawson for allowing me to use three of his ideas for a title of an Elijah biography as chapter-headings; he thereby influenced the other four. And to Dick Lucas for his magnificent sermon in January 1988 on Elijah the suicidal saint; he confirmed many of my hunches, but – more important – he reminded me that it is more important to listen to what the Bible text actually says than to build fanciful speculations upon it.

I am grateful to various publishers and copyright-holders for permission to reprint quotations:
- Hodder & Stoughton for Steve Turner's poem 'History Lesson' from his book *Up to date*;
- Viking Penguin Inc. for James Weldon Johnson's

sermon 'Go down death' from his book *God's Trombones* (© 1927 by the Viking Press Inc. Copyright renewed 1955 by Grace Nail Johnson. All rights reserved);
- Oxford and Cambridge University Presses for the *Ecclesiasticus* extract from the New English Bible Apochrypha, Second Edition © 1970;
- The Evangelical Sisterhood of Mary for Mother Basilea Schlink's *Elijah* prayer.

I should also like to thank everyone else who helped me during the process of writing:
- the Church's Ministry among the Jews' community at Stella Carmel (on Mount Carmel) who put me up (and put up with me) while I researched and wrote; especially Simon Hawthorne and Carol Preston for their stimulating conversations:
- Christine Vasvalingam for long hours of typing and retyping in difficult family circumstances;
- Angie Edge and Marion Machin for patient checking of text and references;
- Shaun Atkins and Nigel Denton for reading the book in draft and suggesting improvements;
- David Jackman, Colin Duriez and their team of readers for making such encouraging editorial comments;
- Nigel Styles and St. Helen's, Bishopsgate's 1988 'Really Arty Weekend' for giving me a fresh look at Elijah at a formative stage; especially Ian Roberts for saving me from at least one embarrassing howler.

Any howlers that remain are despite these friends' best efforts and are entirely my own fault.

Chapter one

The man who changed the weather

In the thirty-eighth year of the reign of King Asa of Judah, Ahab son of Omri became king of Israel, and he ruled in Samaria for twenty-two years. He sinned against the LORD more than any of his predecessors. It was not enough for him to sin like King Jeroboam; he went further and married Jezebel, the daughter of King Ethbaal of Sidon, and worshipped Baal. He built a temple to Baal in Samaria, made an altar for him, and put it in the temple. He also put up an image of the goddess Asherah. He did more to arouse the anger of the LORD, the God of Israel, than all the kings of Israel before him. During his reign Hiel from Bethel rebuilt Jericho. As the LORD had foretold through Joshua son of Nun, Hiel lost his eldest son Abiram when he laid the foundation of Jericho, and his youngest son Segub when he built the gates.

A prophet named Elijah, from Tishbe in Gilead, said to King Ahab, 'In the name of the LORD, the living god of Israel, whom I serve, I tell you that there will be no dew or rain for the next two or three years until I say so.' (1 Kings 16:29 – 17:1)

There was no one else who had devoted himself so completely to doing wrong in the LORD's sight as Ahab – all at the urging of his wife Jezebel. He committed the most shameful sins by worshipping idols, as the Amorites had done, whom the LORD had driven out of the land as the people of Israel advanced. (1 Kings 21:25–26)

Elijah was the same kind of person as we are. He prayed earnestly that there would be no rain, and no rain fell on the land for three and a half years. (James 5:17)

The palace gates were unguarded. Inside the court-yard soldiers, servants, prophets and princes all were a buzz of excitement. The latest consignment of goods had arrived from Sidon.

'Just look at these colours,' gasped the queen's maid as she opened a chest of silks. Like a conjuror pulling a string of handkerchiefs from someone's pocket, she tipped out a rainbow of reds, greens, purples and blues.

Queen Jezebel stepped forward to start modelling a new dress, but another servant caught her eye.

'Your majesty, such jewels!' From a small casket he held up a gold bracelet and several silver necklaces.

She rummaged in the box for herself. She lifted out a handful of precious stones, enjoying the feel of each – its shiny, polished surface; its intricately carved engraving; its solid permanence – before letting them run like grains of sand through her fingers. She spotted an amethyst seal and admired its regal shape. She took it to her husband.

'My lord Ahab, a small trinket from my country,' she said with the note of mixed pride and scorn that Sidon inspired when compared with Israel.

He took it from her without turning. His eyes were on a pair of Arab horses, nervously prancing and pawing the air as their new grooms took hold of the reins.

'Magnificent,' he breathed. 'I must have more. Order them. I want my whole stable fitted out with these Sidonian coursers. And we shall need new chariots to go with them.'

'Er – the expense, Majesty,' murmured his steward Obadiah. 'We cannot expect the queen's father to go on making gifts. For such a large order we shall need to pay, er, handsomely.'

'There is no difficulty,' the queen interrupted. 'My country needs your food. Wheat, barley, vegetables, wine. It's a fair exchange.'

'But the quantities, Majesty.' Obadiah's worried frown persisted. 'We shall need to collect a larger harvest than usual. The rains are not always so generous as in the last year or two.'

Jezebel snorted. 'My god Baal will see to that. Is he not lord of sun and seed, the blesser of crop and herd?'

Another voice cut in; a different voice, rustic, abrupt. 'In the name of Yahweh, the *living* God of *Israel*, I tell you there will be no dew or rain for the next two or three years – until I say so.'

Stunned silence. All eyes turned on the speaker. Who was he? Where had he come from? His voice sounded as if he belonged to Gilead, the rough uplands across the river. His clothes suggested much the same. He was a strange sight among the courtly robes, wearing a shaggy camel-skin, held firm with a leather belt. He looked round from one to the other, holding the eyes of each in turn. Eventually, he shook his head and walked firmly, briskly out.

The silence held. At last Ahab asked, in a low voice, 'Who on earth was that?'

'A prophet of Yahweh, Majesty,' answered Obadiah, 'named Elijah. From Tishbe.'

'Well, after him then!' shouted Jezebel, returning at last to life.

Some guards ran across the courtyard and out through the gate. But Elijah was gone. And no-one could see where.

Samaria

The scene is set in Samaria, about 865 BC. It was the new capital of Israel; a hill-top site bought then built by Omri, father of the present king Ahab. When Ahab succeeded five or six years later, he kept up the prestige building programme.

One of his noteworthy constructions was the so-called 'ivory house' he built for himself. It merited a full account in the official court 'History of the Kings of Israel' (1 Kings 22:39). Archaeological digs in our own century discovered more than 200 ivory plaques or fragments of other ivory decorations. They covered the walls, bed-ends, table-tops, chair-backs. There are carvings of lions, gryphons, sphinxes; following Egyptian fashions, but made in neighbouring Sidon. They are a sign of great prosperity.

The Bible's Book of Kings, on the other hand, is more interested in another of Ahab's building projects – and much less impressed by it. 'He built a temple to Baal . . .'

Ahab was the tenth king of Israel, and from the author's point of view, the worst so far. The unfolding story of the monarchy is a steady decline. 1 Kings opens with David on the throne: a character with spectacular vices to offset his spectacular virtues, but at heart he put first things first and loved God. He handed over to Solomon the wise; another bright start, but sinking into worship of pagan gods under the spell of his pagan wives. His son Rehoboam pitched God's people into partition; the ten northern tribes threw off his repressive regime and turned instead to Jeroboam, one of Solomon's able young officials who had led an abortive coup against him. As long as Jerusalem in the southern kingdom remained the nation's religious centre, Jeroboam could see that his northern kingdom would be hollow. So he built rival shrines at Bethel and Dan. This was not an ignorant mistake; it was disobeying God's instructions and replacing them with something man-made. So his actions became an infamous low-water mark, by which to measure the kings who followed.

All of them failed. Their grim epitaphs read like the verdict on God's day of judgment. Jeroboam's son Nadab: 'Like his father before him, he sinned against the LORD and led Israel into sin' (15:26). He was assassinated and replaced by Baasha: 'Like King Jeroboam before him, he sinned against the LORD and led Israel into sin' (15:34). His successor Elah is bundled into the same condemnation, this time made explicit: 'Because of their idolatry and because they led Israel into sin, Baasha and his son Elah had aroused the anger of the LORD' (16:13). Elah's assassin Zimri lasted only seven days as king, but it was time enough to go the wrong way: 'Like his predecessor Jeroboam he displeased the LORD by his own sins and by leading Israel into sin' (16:19). These were dark days indeed.

Yet worse was to come. The new king Omri, founder of Samaria, plumbed even greater depths: 'Omri sinned against the LORD more than any of his predecessors' (16:25). We do not hear exactly *how* he exceeded the rest, because the next verse merely rings the customary funeral knell: 'Like Jeroboam before him, he aroused the anger of the LORD, the God of Israel, by his sins and by leading the people into sin and idolatry' (16:26).

And so to his son Ahab. It seems scarcely possible to go any lower on the Bible's scale of bad kings. But he does. 'He sinned against the LORD more than any of his predecessors. It was not enough for him to sin like King Jeroboam; . . .' It kept all the other kings busy, but for Ahab it wasn't enough! He had to dig down to a still deeper pit of sinfulness: 'he went further and married Jezebel, the daughter of King Ethbaal of Sidon, and worshipped Baal. He built a temple to Baal in Samaria, made an altar for him, and put it in the temple. He also put up an image of the goddess Asherah. He did more to arouse the anger of the LORD, the God of Israel, than all the kings of Israel before him.'

He married a pagan wife, but Solomon had done that (700 times over!); he worshipped a pagan god, and Solomon had done *that*; the new depth was that he – built a temple to Baal.

Jeroboam's shrines had been meant to honour Israel's GOD, at least in theory. But this was barefaced, brazen homage to Sidon's god. You can almost hear the deliberate effrontery of it in the way the writer records it; you can certainly hear his own shock and horror. 'He built a *temple* (mocking the one true temple in Jerusalem) to *Baal* in *Samaria*' – bad enough; he 'made an altar for him, and put it in the temple' – after time for second thoughts, he really did mean it; 'He also put up an image of the goddess Asherah' – insult on top of injury.

That final insulting flourish gives the game away. Asherah was Baal's wife. Her image appeared in Samaria to please *Ahab's* wife. It says, '*He* built . . . *he* made . . . *he* put up . . .'; but the driving force behind the new inroads Baal made into Israel was the queen. The desperate little epitaph on Ahab in 21:25 says, 'There was no-one else who had devoted himself so completely to doing wrong in the LORD's sight as Ahab – *all at the urging of his wife*'; as one commentator observes, there can hardly be a more shocking verse in the Old Testament. Ahab's sin began not simply in marrying a pagan, but *that* particular pagan: Jeze-baal, daughter of King Ethbaal.

In Ahab's mind the chief consideration was doubtless a marriage of political and economic convenience. It would hitch Israel's waning fortunes on to the wealth and sea-power of Sidon. He wanted to prop up the standard of living somehow. But he found he had married a religious maniac. Her father was a priest of Baal as well as king. She had absorbed his beliefs along with his ruthless methods. She brought 450 prophets of Baal and 400 prophets of Asherah with her, and kept them in her pay (18:19). She made way for them by executing the prophets of Israel's God (18:4) – perhaps the first purely *religious* martyrs in history.

Ahab did not stop her; she was the power behind the throne. There is not even a hint that he raised his voice in protest.

Baal

Of course, if Baal had been *only* a Sidonian cult, he would not have been so dangerous. When we know something is a foreign import, it needs much longer to take hold. But Baal-worship was widespread throughout the Middle East. And Jezebel's Baal-Melqart was just the Sidonian version of something the Israelites already knew and – many of them at least – rather liked.

The people of Israel were constantly warned to stay true to their true God, not to turn aside to their neighbours' gods. Even before they entered the promised land Moses commanded, 'Do not worship other gods, any of the gods of the peoples around you. If you do worship other gods, the LORD's anger will come against you like fire and will destroy you completely, because the LORD your God, who is present with you, tolerates no rivals' (Deuteronomy 6:14,15). Neither God nor Moses thought they were real gods, but they were real rivals for the people's affection and loyalty:

(Deuteronomy 32:37–39)

When the Israelites invaded Canaan, they found a resident 'Baal' (literally 'master', 'owner' or 'husband') worshipped at each shrine or 'high place'. Although under orders to shun or even remove them, they didn't; frequently they found Baal exerting a fatal charm.

Baal-worship is easy for human nature to understand. You give the gods your sacrifice, and they look after you in return. It flatters human vanity: the larger your gift or the louder your chanting, the more impressed the gods will be. Worship is a materialist bargain: you pay your money and get your insurance cover; you do your bit, and then get on with the rest of life.

And as life in primitive societies revolves around the weather, what you're looking to Baal for is the right mix of sun and rain to guarantee the harvest.

Baal is a 'fertility' god. Enter a second feature of Baal-worship. You can speak to the gods in human words, but how can you be sure they've understood? Why not act out your message as well to help them get the point? Now, how do you act out the request, 'Please get on with the business of fertilizing our seeds . . .?' Ah, got it! Baal-shrines engaged 'sacred prostitutes', men and women who openly performed the sex act together to give Baal the right idea. You can imagine the effect of this on the sex life of the people.

Baal-worship appealed to human pride and human lust. It also hardened people's sensitivity and deadened their conscience. How else can we explain its third common feature, human sacrifice? The usual requirement was for a baby or young child to be killed to pacify an angry god or persuade an unwilling one.

This may be what happened in the last verse of 1 Kings 16. When God levelled the walls of Jericho as the Israelites entered the land, he placed the city under a ban:

> *At that time Joshua issued a solemn warning: 'Anyone who tries to rebuild the city of Jericho will be under the LORD's curse.*
> *Whoever lays the foundation will lose his eldest son;*
> *Whoever builds the gates will lose his youngest'.*
> (Joshua 6:26)

Now, in Ahab's time, Hiel tried it. He 'lost' two sons. These may have been building accidents; but, in the Baal-ful atmosphere of the time, they equally may have been 'good luck' sacrifices seeking blessing on the project. A blessing on something that Israel's true God had cursed! That's how little Hiel knew about, or cared about, the LORD.

To all this Jezebel added witchcraft (2 Kings 9:22). The Baal-centres of the Middle-East traded in the occult, as well as bribery, sex and blood.

It is here that I pinch myself awake. This is not just an age-old story of a primitive race. There are uncomfortable echoes of this today. In a British national newspaper at New Year 1988, I read this in the Events column. 'ALLENDALE BAAL FIRE FESTIVAL: A pagan custom to welcome the New Year. Guisers carry blazing barrels on their heads round the village, arriving at the market-square bonfire at midnight.'

A bit of crude fun in a Northumberland village. Not all that significant, perhaps; though the spirit (and here the name) of Baal is not far below the surface at Glastonbury, Stonehenge or other centres of ancient religion.

More widespread, though, are Baal's other rites surviving or reviving in the modern Western world. Superstitious prayers or donations 'for luck'. The 'high priests' of our culture performing sexual coupling on the public screen for money and not for love. Children-in-embryo ripped out of their mothers' wombs and thrown away 'to save distress'. Prime time on breakfast TV given over to astrologers.

'Baal' lives on. And no-one seems the slightest bit disturbed about the anger of the Lord.

The LORD

The word 'LORD' is printed in capitals throughout the Old Testament through an ancient habit. The Hebrew word it translates does not mean 'lord'; it is God's name 'Yahweh' (or 'Jehovah'), which he revealed to Moses (Exodus 3:14).

Later Jewish piety took fright at writing or pronouncing the sacred name, and substituted 'the

Lord'. The capitals indicate that it is a personal name and not a direct translation. But I shall refer to him as Yahweh to save confusion. After all, the name 'Baal' also means the Lord!

By the time of Ahab faith in Yahweh had burned very low. It had been bright in Moses' day, or Joshua's, or David's. The people then had seen him active in their national life; they had heard his words and trusted them. But now – he was still officially honoured as the national God, but in practice most people ignored him. There was real danger that Yahweh-worship would simply collapse under pagan pressure. Then Israel the nation would follow it into oblivion, swallowed up by the surrounding countries.

An outside observer could fairly ask the question Elisha was later to ask: 'Where is Yahweh, the God of Elijah?' (2 Kings 2:14). He was meant to be the God of Israel, but where *was* he? Israel's national fortunes were sinking, their moral standards had sunk. And it appeared that Yahweh had never said a word about it.

It was all very well people like the Bible writer believing and claiming that the kings were arousing Yahweh's anger. But where was it? No blaze of fury. No thunder-bolts. No voice from the heavens. Did he care? Was he there? Was he even alive?

The very questions that people ask today. They ask, and so often they answer no. 'God's not there. God's not alive. No God.' They make three mistakes.

They fail to see that the very silence may be part of God's anger. Part of his punishment on sinful Israel was to allow the terrible sequence of coup and counter-coup among the kings. Israel was already in its fourth unstable dynasty since Solomon, while the other 'half' of God's people, Judah, still had the direct descent from David. Violence, bloodshed and murder on the human stage are not a sign that God doesn't care; rather that he cares enough to let us see the anguish of turning our backs on him. He hopes that this taste of our own medicine will bring us to our senses.

Meanwhile God is not so completely absent as people suppose. Their second mistake is to look only at the events that hit the headlines or the history-books. Yahweh has been banished from the court in Samaria, but that is not the whole of Israel. Hiel may have been corrupted by Ahab's bad example, but there were those who still respected Yahweh's laws. 'Ordinary people' often behave better than their 'leaders'. Wherever true faith continues to shine, that's where Yahweh is.

There was at least one home where he still ruled. In Tishbe in Gilead – rough hill-country, Wales or Scotland as it were, where life was a battle against the elements, and sophisticated Sidonian 'progress' had not arrived. News of Baal's advances must have reached them, though, because one couple dedicated the life of their baby boy to their protest. They called him El-i-yah, 'The real God is Yahweh'. It was an act of brave defiance; like godly parents in Russia or Albania christening their son 'Jesus-is-Lord' or 'Christian'. They reasoned that if Baal demanded child-sacrifice, they would give *their* child to Yahweh's counter-attack. You can be sure they nurtured him with many prayers and patient teaching of the Israelite faith.

They did not make the third mistake – which is to imagine that, because God has not unleashed the punishment he warned of, he never will. It was only 20 years or so since the death of Baasha and Elah. Yahweh pronounced their death sentence through the prophet Jehu as capital punishment for sinful kingship (6:1–12). Simply because he had not (yet) taken similar action against Omri or Ahab, it was perilously foolish to conclude that he was unable to.

If Elijah's parents prayed for their boy to help show Yahweh's arm and conquer Baal, it was a prayer he took up and used.

A prophet

There's an old saying about Jesus: 'God had one son, and he made him a preacher'. God's spokesmen play a critical part in the strategy of his kingdom. When God wants to announce his next move, to pass sentence, to teach, to comfort, he calls a speaker. The Bible's pages are full of God's prophets, and a goodly fellowship they are. Prophets still speak today when they bring God's word to bear on a question or need. Not all Christians are prophets, but many of us speak 'prophetically' when God uses us to give help, encouragement and comfort (1 Corinthians 14:3).

But of all the thousands of prophetic utterances, Elijah's here must be the most dramatic. Was there ever such an entrance or opening line on stage? As a spiritual stun-grenade, it is devastating. It has been called the shortest sermon in history. It is not a sermon as we understand sermons today: institutionalized in a pulpit, from where it rains sweet reason down on the rows of polite listeners. *This* sermon was more of an interruption, a shout on the run, an insult. To be precise, it was a curse.

It certainly *is* short – a single sentence. But each phrase, each word brims with meaning. Years of prayer, learning, reflection, pain and indignation have been poured into it. In this one little capsule Elijah and God have concentrated the unanswerable check to Baal.

It starts with a double oath, and finishes with the most astonishing weather forecast.

1. First, the oath:
(A) *In the name of Yahweh, the living God of Israel*. Elijah begins his sermon with the ascription, 'In the name of God'. He is speaking for Yahweh. His words are the Lord's. Though the word 'I' is prominent in the remaining three parts of his message, he is not self-opinionated. He claims God's authority for what he is about to say.

His opening word is also a missile, a javelin hurled into the enemy camp. In the palace of Baal, he dares to speak of Yahweh and for Yahweh. He will not leave Baal to rule unchallenged. Just the name of Yahweh, as now the name of Jesus, is a weapon to fling at demonic powers wherever they are in place.

For Yahweh is the *living* God. You may not have seen him lately. But he's here; and alive; and active; and powerful. This makes Elijah's word more deadly than a spear. It's a grenade or mine to explode Baal to pieces. It's a mocking taunt. Our God's alive – so sorry about yours. Baal is a godling made in man's image, a product of human imagination. He doesn't even exist.

A poor little dead thing. Brush him off.

He shouldn't be here anyway. Yahweh is the *God of Israel*. The people of God belong exclusively to God by a solemn, binding agreement. In the Old Testament, agreed with Abraham, it is applied to each male of the kingdom through the mark of circumcision. In the New Testament it is signed, sealed and delivered by Jesus' death-blood, poured on to each member of the kingdom through the shower of baptism. No other God has any right to be present – Baal, sex, money, self, ambition, respectability, family, the other things we turn into idols and crave for. They're not admitted. Tell them to get lost. Easier said than done? Yes, but the other half of the oath helps.

(B) *Whom I serve*. Here is the oath of allegiance; the covenant-promise reaffirmed. Where has Elijah found the courage to confront the king, and (more to the point) the queen? From being Yahweh's servant. We may not all be prophets, but we are all God's servants. When we understand that our whole life belongs to God, that we serve and worship him through every activity, he begins truly to master us. He fills our entire horizon. And his enemies fall into their proper, rather puny, perspective. Any thought, word or deed that cuts against his will or interests is out of the question; any motive, activity or relationship; and pressure, power or law, however high its source. If I am God's servant, I obey him rather than any human authority that goes against him.

I am Yahweh's servant. That was Elijah's credential and badge. It was his whole identity. From the cradle he had learnt to see himself as being on this planet to do Yahweh's bidding, and so to be a model of his lifestyle. Elijah defined himself as Yahweh's servant. It would be a good way for us to define ourselves too. It would give us the nerve and the muscle to achieve something useful for God's kingdom.

2. And so to the weather forecast:
(A) *I tell you that there will be no dew or rain.* Elijah brings the challenge to Baal to an acid test. He's supposed to be a god of fertility; well, let's see how he gets on without any water. Jezebel's Sidonians pictured him as a sun-god; all right, if you worship him, the sun is all you'll get.

As Elijah has already said, though, this is Yahweh's forecast, not his own. He didn't hit on the idea himself as a neat punishment to fit the crime. He read it in the Bible. He mulled over God's words in Israel's charter deeds.

So then, obey the commands that I have given you today; love Yahweh your God and serve him with all your heart. If you do, he will send rain on your land when it is needed, in the autumn and in the spring, so that there will be corn, wine and olive-oil for you, and grass for your cattle. You will have all the food you want. Do not let yourselves be led away from Yahweh to worship and serve other gods. If you do, Yahweh will become angry with you. He will hold back the rain, and your ground will become too dry for crops to grow. Then you will soon die there, even though it is a good land that he is giving you.
(Deuteronomy 11:13–17)

And again:

> *If you do evil and reject Yahweh, he will bring on you disaster, confusion, and trouble in everything you do, until you are quickly and completely destroyed. . . No rain will fall, and your ground will become as hard as iron. Instead of rain, Yahweh will send down duststorms and sandstorms until you are destroyed.*
> (Deuteronomy 28:20,23–24)

Did God mean it? Elijah couldn't bear the thought of Yahweh being ridiculed and despised for making empty threats he couldn't carry out. His heart burned with shame and anger at Ahab and Hiel, and countless other Israelites, sticking two fingers up at God's warnings. How dare they say, 'I don't care'? How could they escape, now they had trampled all over Yahweh's long-suffering patience? He realized that his anger was a faint afterpang or Yahweh's own.

This stirred him to prayer. James tells us that he prayed *earnestly*. James's exact phrase is 'he prayed in prayer'. It is a Jewish way of saying he prayed hard. He prayed and prayed. He prayed real prayers. He prayed to the power and intensity of prayer. O Lord, this is desperate. O Lord, hear me. O Lord, do something! Lord, don't say no. You can't. You mustn't. Please!

As he prayed and brooded and hurt, his conviction became clear that *he* was God's weather-forecaster. Surely now was the day for Yahweh's warnings to take effect.

(B) *No dew or rain for the next two or three years until I say so.* Perhaps our sceptical generation needs reminding that this is not a fairy-tale, but a record of history. Modern research has established that there *were* three-year droughts in the second millennium BC as the African deserts caused shifting patterns in the neighbouring rainbelts. And the ancient Greek historian Menander records a one-year drought in neighbouring Sidon during the reign of Ahab's contemporary and father-in-law, Ethbaal.

But Elijah foretold this one. He saw that it must last two or three years to fulfil the Deuteronomy warnings. He felt Yahweh had appointed him the monitor of Israel's response. So, on the human level, his judgment of when the people repented would give the say-so for the rains to return.

What magnificent faith! He seems to have conquered every thought of 'supposing it doesn't work!' But then his faith was fed on God's words, rightly understood and rightly applied. The reason why we could not command a drought over Manchester, say, is not our lack of faith or the soggy climate, but that there is no such curse in the New Testament.

God-sent drought was a punishment specified for Yahweh's Old Testament people. Elijah's Bible-taught faith, however, is an example to us all.

Elijah

A final section to the chapter; but there is no more we can say with certainty.

Everything we know about Elijah at this stage of the story has already emerged.

We have deduced a little about his parents. But

we don't know their names, or their tribe, or the rest of their family. Some Jews interpreted Elijah's lack of a family-tree as meaning that he was an angel. That would immediately put him beyond the reach of mere mortals like us. But James insists that 'Elijah was the same kind of person as we are' (5:17). Any of us can learn to be an Elijah – not the weather-forecaster with atmospheric stage-effects, perhaps; but a faithful servant of the living God, certainly.

We know Elijah was a prophet, but nothing about his call or early training. So much the better. It doesn't matter how or where we were brought up and educated. It doesn't matter what our subject or job is. It doesn't matter how or when we became a Christian. There are no specially favourable countries, colleges or formulae. We are simply called to join Elijah in the service corps and fulfil our own ministry, whatever it happens to be.

I'm assuming Elijah was unmarried and childless, but we don't know. We do know what his costume was – the animal skin with leather belt – but nothing else about his appearance. We don't know his age. In this book I imagine him passing from 40 to 55 through the 15 or so years that the events cover (roughly 865–850 BC). But that need not exclude you if you are younger or older. The pattern unravelled in the next few chapters of training – prime – change of life – retirement – heaven, is a cycle that we have all begun and all still need to learn.

For further reflection

1. What echoes of Ahab's Samaria can you detect in your own country today? How do you think the writer of Kings would sum up your present regime?

2. What do you think God is wanting to say or do to your country as a whole? How might he want you (and any Christian fellowship you belong to) to take part in his plans?

3. How would you rate yourself as a servant of God? How can you be sure of developing into a more effective one?

Chapter two

The man who disappeared

Then the LORD said to Elijah, 'Leave this place and go east and hide yourself near the brook of Cherith, east of the Jordan. The brook will supply you with water to drink, and I have commanded ravens to bring you food there.'

Elijah obeyed the LORD's command, and went and stayed by the brook of Cherith. He drank water from the brook, and ravens brought him bread and meat every morning and every evening. After a while the brook dried up because of the lack of rain.

Then the LORD said to Elijah, 'Now go to the town of Zarephath, near Sidon, and stay there. I have commanded a widow who lives there to feed you.' So Elijah went to Zarephath, and as he came to the gate of the town, he saw a widow gathering firewood. 'Please bring me a drink of water,' he said to her. And as she was going to get it, he called out, 'And please bring me some bread, too.'

She answered, 'By the living LORD your God I swear that I haven't got any bread. All I have is a handful of flour in a bowl and a drop of olive-oil in a jar. I came here to gather some firewood to take back home and prepare what little I have for my

son and me. That will be our last meal, and then
we will starve to death.'

'Don't worry,' Elijah said to her. 'Go ahead and
prepare your meal. But first make a small loaf from
what you have and bring it to me, and then prepare
the rest for you and your son. For this is what the
LORD, the God of Israel, says: "The bowl will not
run out of flour or the jar run out of oil before the
day that I, the LORD, send rain." '

The widow went and did as Elijah had told her,
and all of them had enough food for many days.
As the LORD had promised through Elijah, the bowl
did not run out of flour nor did the jar run out of
oil.

Some time later the widow's son fell ill; he got
worse and worse, and finally he died. She said to
Elijah, 'Man of God, why did you do this to me?
Did you come here to remind God of my sins and
so cause my son's death?'

'Give the boy to me,' Elijah said. He took the
boy from her arms, carried him upstairs to the room
where he was staying, and laid him on the bed. Then
he prayed aloud, 'O LORD my God, why have you
done such a terrible thing to this widow? She has
been kind enough to take care of me, and now you
kill her son!' Then Elijah stretched himself out on
the boy three times and prayed. 'O LORD my God,
restore this child to life!' The LORD answered
Elijah's prayer; the child started breathing again and
revived.

Elijah took the boy back downstairs to his mother
and said to her, 'Look, your son is alive!'

She answered, 'Now I know that you are a man
of God and that the LORD really speaks through
you!' (1 Kings 17:2–24)

'I tell you this,' Jesus added, *'a prophet is never welcomed in his home town.*

'Listen to me: it is true that there were many widows in Israel during the time of Elijah, when there was no rain for three and a half years and a severe famine spread throughout the whole land. Yet Elijah was not sent to anyone in Israel, but only to a widow living in Zarephath in the territory of Sidon. And there were many people suffering from a dreaded skin-disease who lived in Israel during the time of the prophet Elisha; yet not one of them was healed, but only Naaman the Syrian.'
(Luke 4:24–27)

'Don't just stand there,' Ahab shouted. 'Fetch horses. Pursue him all the way to . . . *where* did you say, Obadiah?'

'Tishbe, Majesty. In Gilead.'

'Very well. You heard. Call at every village on the way. Check that he's not hiding.'

Grooms ran to harness horses and attach chariots. A platoon of soldiers gathered the provisions they would need. And in a swirl of dust they left.

Three days later they were back. There was no sign of him. No-one had seen him. They had ransacked every house in Tishbe. The villagers swore that they had heard nothing from him since he set off in high excitement a week earlier. All the evidence bore them out.

'A curse on the man. He must have gone another way. Try north, south, west. And this time, *find* him.'

More soldiers, horses, chariots sped out on the hunt. Over the next few weeks, they all came back empty-handed. Elijah had gone to ground without trace.

Ahab stamped the dust in irritation. 'He can't vanish into thin air. He's not an angel of Yahweh, is he?' He regretted the words at once and smiled nervously at his wife. 'Begging your pardon for mentioning the name, dearest.'

She shrugged. 'The answer's obvious. He must have crossed a border. Send to our neighbours: Judah, Edom, Egypt, Moab, Ammon, Syria, Philistia. Make them search. High and low. Come, I'll draw up a document they must seal to swear that they have looked in every city and village. I want that man brought back to me.'

'And your father, my dear. I'll send to him as well.'

'It is hardly necessary. *Naturally* King Ethbaal would never harbour a prophet of Yahweh.'

The messengers went. And one by one they returned. Their scrolls were correctly signed and sealed; but still no Elijah.

Jezebel lashed out like a frustrated snake. 'All right, then. Get his friends instead. Track down every single prophet of Yahweh and kill them.'

Soldiers turned and moved wearily on this latest errand of spite. The sun had blazed relentlessly for nearly a year now. They were hot, sweaty, itchy.

Obadiah overheard their marching orders, and his blood ran cold. Despite his high position at court, he worshipped Yahweh. He made no show of it, he dreaded Jezebel noticing and taking exception. But he could not stand by and watch the extermination of his country's prophets without doing something to help.

He knew where the two nearest 'schools' or

communities of prophets lived. He could at least send warning to them. But who to send? There was no-one to trust. He would have to go himself. After dark. Travelling as silently as he could, he reached them before Jezebel's executioners. He led them to well hidden caves near a spring that was still flowing. During the months while Jezebel's purge lasted, he smuggled out supplies of food. He was terrified that he would be discovered; as the drought seared into its second year, the palace's stores of food became scarcer, and he had to explain why the inmates' rations kept getting smaller.

The pagans all round him moaned and swore. Obadiah, though, was secretly delighted. It was a blow, although a savage one, for Yahweh. They had ignored him, flouted his laws to his face. And now Elijah had unleashed his judgment on them. Drought and famine are always harsh in their effects; but a drought sent and meant by God, he reasoned, will surely lead to good.

Two or three years

There is a remarkable passage in the New Testament which understands our own age as in some ways similar to Elijah's drought – Revelation 11:1–6. It lasts the same time (three and a half years), but the number takes on symbolic undertones of being evil and only temporary – it is half the number of perfect completeness. It is an age in which the true worshippers are displaced and threatened by the heathen trampling the Holy City and the temple's outer courts. But God's chosen witnesses are kept safe; they breathe fire on their enemies. They have authority to shut off the rain. And their task is to proclaim God's message.

Revelation characterizes the Church and its preachers as modern Elijahs. His task too was to proclaim God's message. He had already begun. But God used three and a half years to give that first sermon a chance to sink in and take root. He had other plans for Elijah like training him for the next message.

Elijah could not tell in advance how long this course would last as a student in God's training college. A *mature* student, if we take him to be already middle-aged. As Christians, we never reach an end of learning, and every stage of life proves a training-ground for the next or a later one. Mid-life is especially apt for taking stock of God's call, and perhaps taking a fresh direction to pursue it in the years that are left.

At all events, 1 Kings 17 shows Elijah spending the next three years as God's college student. They were 'hidden' years – literally hidden from Jezebel's murderous search-parties. Elijah may have expected further high-level confrontations at court. He must have wondered whether God had forgotten or sacked him. One national prophecy in three years is hardly a heavy work-load. But effective work for God takes years of preparation. The great contest on Carmel that was to come needed three years' training.

Most of us spend most of our lives doing pretty humdrum, unremarkable things. The schedule repeats itself routinely day after day. We may sometimes feel that in the light of eternity it is a bit of a waste of time. We may hanker for a calling more obviously in the cut and thrust of God's front line. But provided we have asked God to put us where he wants us, and followed such leading as he's given, nothing is wasted. It may be a small-scale, uneventful period in our life. But God is wanting to use every experience to equip us for something else later.

If you long to be an Elijah of 'Carmelite' proportions, you need first to go through the training school of Cherith and Zarephath. If God cannot trust you to be faithful and make the most of where you are now, how can he let you loose on the scale you dream of? Any God-given ministry must start small, in order to grow and develop. Arthur Blessitt is now a celebrated missionary to the world, carrying a cross and preaching in every country that will admit him; he began as a child by explaining the gospel to his pet dog!

Cherith (verses 2–7)

The chapter gives us three short extracts from Elijah's training course; perhaps one taken from each year.

First, God sends him to the brook of Cherith, with the instruction to hide. This part was easy. Tishbe is on the Cherith; this was Elijah's own neck of the woods. He'd played there as a child. He knew every hiding-place with his eyes closed. He needed to; when Ahab's bloodhounds came sniffing and scenting, he had to lie low.

This was where it became harder. He mustn't

trek upstream and home for a good square meal and a comfy bed. No-one must know where he is. The instructions are unorthodox, but crystal clear. 'The brook will supply you with water to drink, and I have commanded ravens to bring you food there.' The first part of the course is some kind of endurance test, out in the open, alone, with no reassuring back-pack.

That was all God said on the published syllabus. But as with any good curriculum, he had a host of lessons for Elijah to learn in the process. Here are four of the most immediate; others will emerge as time goes on.

1. Theology: learning to grasp a bigger vision of God
Fancy using birds as divine waiters! God is not stumped for lack of people. If no other person must see Elijah or know where he is, well, an animal can do the job. Yahweh is lord of the whole creation.

He kept those ravens busy. Twice a day, every day, for up to a year; carrying a man-size meal each time. That is some airlift! It was either a lot of trips for a small squadron of birds; or he called up large reserves of ravens.

'Not ravens!' Elijah must have shuddered. He knew of them, as members of the crow family, as 'unclean', non-kosher, unfit to eat (Leviticus 11:15; Deuteronomy 14:14). They tend to feed on carrion, offal and rotting matter. But now he had to eat what had been in their beaks, or starve. We can easily become prejudiced, over-particular, exclusive when we go beyond God's laws into our own rules for daily living.

2. Self-mastery: learning to live alone

Those once despised ravens must have seemed welcome companions in the long months with no human friendship. It's not 'natural', and not God's long-term plan, for people to live as recluses. 'It is not good for the man to live alone.' Or as John Donne put the same truth, 'No man is an island. . .'. Yet there are times when God tips us out of the nest: when we first leave home, our first job, posted overseas, being redundant, widowed, bereaved. Handicap may hit us, especially in old age; we become deaf or blind or housebound. Suddenly we lose the familiar props, the people we always turn to. We have only ourselves to rely on, only ourselves to live with. At least, ourselves *and God*. That is the point of the training: learning to draw on God's company *for ourselves*; turning loneliness from a scourge and phobia (*the* disease of our times, indeed) into a blessing.

Religion has been defined, most inadequately, as 'what a man does with his solitude'. But it has this fragment of the truth. God seems to include this development of the self-life in the training programme for people with a prophetic ministry of understanding his will and explaining it to others. Part of their calling is to listen and talk to God alone. The sooner they start, the better.

3. Simple lifestyle: learning to be content with enough

This was an austerity diet, but not a starvation diet. God saw to it that Elijah had enough to eat. Two plain, adequate, regular meals each day: bread and meat, carbohydrate and protein, morning and evening. *Just* two – no midday snack, no after-dinner mints. And just water to drink – no wine or minerals or fruit-juice. Healthy but unexciting. One of the difficulties of simple living is the lack of variety. How Elijah must have craved sometimes for vegetables or flavouring or cake!

There is no particular virtue in denying ourselves the rich abundance of what God's earth produces when it is readily available. But when resources run short, he expects us to live simply so that others may simply live. Elijah's experience teaches us how little we can live on. God gave him all he needed, perhaps not all he would have liked. This questions the size of our freezers; the artificial food and drink we consume (proved to be less nourishing than their containers); the way we throw good food, paper, cardboard, metal, glass, clothes and oil away without taking them to be recycled; the electricity, gas and petrol we guzzle in unnecessary gadgets, central heating or car journeys. Elijah could teach us a thing or two about walking and running. The purpose of this self-discipline should include helping others. God does not send birds to feed starving humans today, because he expects *us* to do it.

4. Faith: *learning to trust God for everything*
Most people in the developed world usually know where the next meal's coming from. It'll be out of Mum's oven in the kitchen, or out of a packet if I'm cooking it, or from the Chinese take-away. And, of course, if we're Christians we'll say grace over it and acknowledge that it's also, if you go back to basics, from God.

Just occasionally God checks whether we really mean it. Jesus taught us to pray, 'Give us today the food we need.' Elijah had to do so in all earnest. So did the Israelites in the desert (Exodus 16). So have some Christians in places hit by famine, or in 'faith missions', where no regular income is guaranteed. All have tended to find that God supplies just enough for today – no left-overs, or there would be no need for faith tomorrow.

God calls all Christians to live on faith (2 Corinthians 5:7). So his training for all of us includes lessons in trusting him to provide. Not food, necessarily – sometimes it's money, or clothes, or work, or somewhere to live; a vital piece of equipment. They all belong to God in the last resort; they are his to give. And as with Elijah – water from the stream, food by carrier-raven – they usually come in a special blend of natural means and supernatural control.

Not that we can turn 'The Lord will provide' into a pat formula. Even that can in time send our faith to sleep. Elijah lived with permanent uncertainty about the future. The ravens may have been as reliable as clockwork, but Cherith began to run out. As the sun sucked up the vapour, the brook gradually slowed to a trickle, then stood still in puddles, which inched inwards and inwards. Finally nothing; the drinking water was finished. And only then did Yahweh speak again.

Zarephath (verses 8–16)

Elijah's training teaches us not only the simple lifestyle, but also the provisional lifestyle. Be ready to move on; maybe at short notice. God doesn't want us to become so attached to any place or people or home that we mistake them for our real home, which is him. He doesn't want any routine to become a rut from which we cannot move.

So now, for year two, as it were, he moves Elijah 75 miles north-west to Zarephath. Many college students spend part of their course in what is called, slightly oddly, a 'placement'. The idea is that they are 'placed' among ordinary people to put all that ivory tower theory into practice; to see if it works 'in real life' and on the job.

Zarephath was Elijah's placement. In many ways it could hardly have been a bigger change. Instead of the country brook, he lived next to the vast Mediterranean. Instead of the open air, he had a roof over his head. And after all that loneliness he had people to talk to; he was living in with a family – a widow and her child – where he could be some use, and a man about the house.

And yet – same drought, same shortages, same God-tutor to learn from. And again, a flow of lessons to absorb; some were more of the same, others entirely new.

The theology course continued; we never finish learning to grasp a bigger view of God. Yahweh has another chuckle up his sleeve as he leads Elijah into this lesson. Last year it was ravens, to show he can use even 'unclean' animals. This year it is Lebanon, to show he loves 'unclean' people. Now, would you choose Lebanon as a safe sanctuary for a precious hostage? The name was different then, of course – Sidon – but it was the same country, and just as threatening to Elijah. If it all sounded rather idyllic two paragraphs ago, to Elijah it felt like out of the frying pan into the fire. And that's how it was meant to feel, even down to the name:

Zarephath means 'a smelter's crucible'. God had further refining, re-shaping, training to do on Elijah; as he has on us.

The prickly fact was that Sidon was Jezebel's homeland. Zarephath is a mere eight or nine miles down the coast from the town of Sidon where her father lived. He was the arch-priest of Baal. The 'joke' was that God had buried his chief strike-weapon right under the enemy's nose. It was a brilliant tactic; the last place Ahab would think of looking.

Yet there was more to learn than that. Elijah had to come to terms with this stubborn fact that Yahweh had sent him to lodge with a fellow-countrywoman of Jezebel's; to share a home with her and learn to care about her. By being a Sidonian she was automatically a non-Israelite; therefore a Gentile. Yahweh was asking him to share life with someone outside the covenant. (At least, that is the natural assumption, which I am making. It is possible she was an Israelite in exile, which could explain her respect for Yahweh. But the implication of Jesus' words in Luke 4:26–27 weighs against this.)

God made his old bargain with one nation-race, so that they could be a demonstration model to the rest of humanity. They interpreted favour as favouritism, and concluded that God was only interested in them. It is a universal human failing to set up a barrier between 'my sort of people' and the also-rans. A great deal of the learning God has to put us through is to *unlearn* this prejudice; to discover that the also-rans are also humans, and that God loves them as much as he loves us. In his programme for you and me, this is what difficult relations, school-fellows, teachers, bosses, work-mates, even fellow Christians, are for.

The faith course continued too; it always does, in one form or another. Here the test was the same: what shall we eat tomorrow? But the answer was beautifully, totally different. Who says God is dull or lacks imagination? Who says he always does things to a set pattern? This time, no brook, no ravens. Just a handful of flour and a drop of olive-oil. *Every day* a handful of flour and a drop of oil. Even when we went wild yesterday and licked up every last grain of flour and glob of oil, there's still a handful and a drop today. Give us today our daily bread. A prayer for every Christian every day.

The new course was in community living. Elijah needed to learn more of how to get on with people, as well as how to be a loner. Two profound lessons come up to the surface.

One was to share resources. Verse 13 leaves Bible commentators uneasy, because it sounds so callously selfish. The widow has just announced she is preparing her final, funeral meal before she dies; there is only enough for her and the boy. 'Don't worry,' Elijah seems to breeze. 'Go ahead and prepare your meal. But not till you have first made a small loaf for me.' At least he has the grace only to want a *small* loaf! But he is speaking already in the knowledge of verse 14 and of the faith it generates. Yahweh has said, 'The bowl will not run out of flour or the jar run out of oil.' They are the bowl and jar he has commandeered to feed Elijah (verse 9). Elijah is to be part of the family. So he has a share at the family table.

Sharing resources is a golden key to families, communities, Christian fellowships; and it can apply far more widely still. Why have five hair-driers or lawn-mowers or photocopiers when one could be shared? Why do five people all need paid jobs when four could support one to do vital voluntary work? Yet when we fence part of our lives off with a burglar alarm labelled 'mine, mine, mine', we stunt and damage the community we belong to.

The second lesson stems from the first. Elijah has no resources to share, so has to learn simply to receive. And as that exactly mirrors our stance before God, it is a good lesson to learn. But a hard one; so many of us would rather be in the credit position, where we are the capable, all-sufficient ones, with others gateful to us. It comes far less easily to admit that we are empty-handed and utterly dependent. Elijah's male pride took knock after knock as he had to . . . beg . . . from a woman . . . who was a poor widow . . . with only enough for herself.

The widow's son died (verses 17–24)

Crisis. Alarm. Panic. After months of successful survival on the miracle bowl and jar and the small water-ration from the town well, Hiram (let's call him) fell ill. Elijah and Astarte (let's call her) watched in despair as medicine failed, prayer failed, and finally life itself failed.

Elijah had grown fond of young Hiram and wept. But rather than comfort each other in their grief, Astarte rounded on him. 'This is your fault,' she wailed. 'You and your God. You've come here and shown him my sins. And now he's done this to punish me. Why have you been so cruel to me?'

Conflicting thoughts raced in Elijah's mind. He longed to defend himself against such an unfair accusation. It wasn't *his* fault; he'd worked hard to save Hiram. Then there was her misunderstanding about sin – strange and revealing how when disaster hits us, our conscience immediately reads it as God giving us what we deserve for our sins. The theology student wanted to put her right and sort her out.

But this wasn't the moment. Every good training programme builds in experiences like this where the learner is suddenly out on his own and up against it. In a driving test it is the emergency stop. The trainee surgeon has to take charge of her first operation. The student pastor finds himself counselling someone in real need. This was Elijah's practical test. Everything he'd learned so far was called into play.

He took the light ten-year-old body from Astarte's arms, climbed up the outside staircase to his room on the roof, and laid Hiram on the bed. He prayed. What else can you do in a disaster but pray? But this prayer included a new depth, and a new urgency. Astarte's words had in effect been a challenge to Yahweh and all that Elijah stood for. This stung him to pray earnestly as he had for Israel, and even more earnestly. Verse 21 speaks of Elijah stretching himself; God gave the faith to stretch Elijah's grasp of prayer beyond where it had grown so far.

1. Praying alone (verse 19)
We may say we spend time alone with God in prayer, but it is worth checking ruthlessly. It is easy

to kid ourselves. Without it our spiritual growth will be lopsided. Leonard Ravenhill overstated the case with his epigram, 'The secret of praying is praying in secret.' Jesus attaches special grace 'where two or three come together' to pray (Matthew 18:19–20) – a married couple, a family, close friends, a home group, a Christian Union. But equally, he expects each member to pray alone as well; in words reminiscent of Elijah, he instructs, 'when you pray, go to your room, close the door, and pray to your Father, who is unseen. And your Father, who sees what you do in private, will reward you' (Matthew 6:6). Elijah meant business with God and wanted the reward of private prayer. The great advantage of praying alone is that you are uninterrupted and able to concentrate.

2. Honest feelings (verse 20)
Elijah lets his emotions fly in what must be one of the rudest, bluntest prayers in Scripture. He prays out loud, 'Yahweh, why have you done such a terrible thing to this widow? She has been kind enough to take care of me, and now you kill her son!' He accuses God of being less Christian than Astarte, and of murder! He is bitter, sarcastic and totally honest.

I hear the voices of my upbringing tutting, 'You mustn't talk to God like that!' But why not? Many of the Psalms sound like this, too. God knows that's what we're thinking. When we realize he can stand hearing it without being shocked, we shall grow. He wants us to spit our anguish out, so that he can deal with it and heal it. If we nurse it inside and pretend to be pious, it remains and festers.

3. Concern for the victim (verse 20)

What has really got to Elijah is Astarte's distress at losing her only means of support. His indignation is on behalf of 'this widow'. So much of our praying is deeply selfish. Even when we pray for other people, our requests can be for our own convenience or gratification. 'Lord, please make my supervisor overlook my shoddy work.' 'Make Deborah easier to get on with.' 'Please convert Tom because he's such a nice person; it would be wonderful to have him as a Christian.' God wants to lead us on to love our neighbour as ourself in how we pray for him.

4. Close identification (verse 21)

Elijah's bodily 'stretching' is an extension of this concern for the person he is praying for. It is a strange thought that a grown man has to stretch himself to cover the body of a small child; you'd think rather he would hunch himself up. At all events he lay on top of the lifeless body, covering face, arms, legs with his. As he did so, he must have thought, 'Here we go again. One more "unclean" notion (Numbers 19:16) that God has brought me to see in perspective.' When the corpse is someone you love and care about, someone you count as your own family, you want to touch them, whatever the ritual inconvenience.

The basic meaning of Elijah's action is clear. 'Lord, I want you to overshadow this lad and bring him to birth again – all of him. Make him whole. If only you could take my breath and warmth and transfer them into him. I would be willing to lay down my life for him.' Sometimes in prayer we feel so deeply we can't put it all into words. But a gesture, a posture can say it for us. I have lain, knelt, run, jumped, laughed, yelled in prayer. The fellow I shared digs with as a student once ripped his pyjamas while praying; he was energetically punching the air while exhorting the Lord to beat down the devil and all his forces!

5. *Think big (verse 21)*

It is easy with Christian hindsight to miss the enormity of what Elijah was asking. People have rightly observed that he was definite in his request: not just a vague 'I feel so miserable' or 'Help us' or 'Please do something', but a precise, measurable 'Yahweh, restore this child to life!' The real point is that this is the first resurrection in the Bible. Elijah was asking God to do something new; there was nothing in print to say that this was his line of business. As we shall see in a moment, there is good reason to think that God gave Elijah assurance that he was praying in the right direction. But this time there were no laws or guarantees in Deuteronomy to cling on to.

So this is where Elijah's prayer outreaches his earlier experience. It is the stretching of faith to cross frontiers, to conquer new territory and occupy it for God. Missionaries who take the good news where it has never been before pray with this kind of bold imagination. God is not limited, he can do anything except go against his own will or character. So why not pray big? It's a compliment to God.

> Thou art coming to a King;
> Large petitions with thee bring;
> For his grace and power are such,
> None can ever ask too much.
> (John Newton)

Having said that, should we pray today for the dead to return to life? It is not a ridiculous idea. It worked for Elijah and Elisha, and the New Testament does not dismiss their experience; it records them in the annals of faith (Hebrews 11:35). Jesus also raised a widow's son; a synagogue official's daughter; and a close personal friend. He gave the twelve apostles authority to do the same (Matthew 10:8); both Peter and Paul did. However, it was always a rare, special wonder; just eight instances in the whole Bible, apart from Jesus' own return from death. Reports of similar resurrections since New Testament times are few and far between, and difficult to substantiate with certainty. There is a good New Testament reason why this should be. Until Jesus' own resurrection, God had not fully revealed what happens after death. Jesus 'has ended the power of death and through the gospel has revealed immortal life' (2 Timothy 1:10). We now know that 'Everyone must die once, and after that be judged by God' (Hebrews 9:27). The apostles nowhere teach us to interfere with this normal course of events. Christians, in particular, wouldn't thank us for bringing them back to earth; they have gone to 'be with Christ, which is a far better thing' (Philippians 1:23). We shall indeed be raised from death, but in a new and better kingdom (1 Corinthians 15:20–28).

This life is the time for coming alive spiritually by turning to God. That was the point of this training for Elijah. He was learning to bring spiritual revival to Israel, not to become a travelling resuscitator.

6. Keep praying (verse 21)

As Christian students, we used to encourage one another, when passing in the street, with the coded message, 'K.p., K.p.' This was nothing to do with a certain brand of salted peanuts. It stood for 'Keep praying'! We were impressed with the need to persevere in prayer.

My son often announces what he plans to buy when he has saved enough pocket money. Some ideas last only a day or two, before giving way to the next craze. Others, however, persist. We hear of nothing else but this marvellous toy. Excitement mounts with the coins. At last we can afford the trip to the shop, and the treasured desire comes home. It's really his.

It's much the same with our prayers. Many are passing fancies. The Lord is in the ones where he plants such a strong longing and certainty that we will not give up. He purifies our desires and strengthens our faith. After one 'false start', Elijah must have been tempted to think, 'Oh, give up. I'm asking the impossible.' But he didn't; he stretched himself out and prayed again, and a third time. Sometimes God delays his answer in order to teach us. It is the only way we will learn that *God alone* can answer our prayer, and *prayer alone* can reach him. You may have deep prayer concerns and longings, which have passed the test of time: for your children, or 'godchildren', to become mature Christians; for the conversion of a spouse or other close friend; for a lively Christian fellowship to take root in a school, or housing estate, or remote part of the world. Like Elijah, you need to keep praying. It may be more than three times; perhaps 365 times a year, not just for three and a half years but 35 years. It won't often take that long, but if it does, so be it. Elijah kept praying till Yahweh answered; the child started breathing again and revived.

One feels that Astarte's words in verse 24 that end the chapter are definitely an abridged version of her outpourings. The Bible only records what's important. But this sentence must have sounded like a fanfare of trumpets to Elijah. He'd passed – with honours. His training, the formal period at least, was done.

The words also revealed that he had indeed been able to contribute something to the small household in the drought. Not food and drink, maybe, but something far more important. As Yahweh's servant, his steady witness and then his action in the crisis had led Astarte from mere awareness of God ('the living Yahweh *your* God', verse 12), through personal admission of sin (verse 18) to first-hand faith and certainty ('Now I know . . .'). His training had taught him how to be Yahweh's instrument in persuading one woman that he was the true God. Now he must do it for a whole nation.

The word of Yahweh came. . .

The chapter has three scenes, but one star actor. It is not Elijah. The real hero of the action is God, or, as it is presented here, his word. The Good News Bible's 'Then the Lord said' masks the dramatic phrasing of the Hebrew, 'The word of Yahweh came' (verses 2,8), 'the word of Yahweh in your mouth is true' (verse 24).

In Old Testament thought Yahweh's word is a living force, able to change whatever it hits. Here it takes the initiative at each new departure; it comes and finds Elijah; it tells him all that he needs to know for now, one step at a time; it proves right and true every time, the one reliable anchor when the outlook is at its bleakest. God's word brings clear directions ('go east', 'go to Zarephath') when human wits don't know where to turn for the best. It offers reassuring promises ('The brook will supply you', 'The bowl will not run out') when our usual resources have run out and we're on the verge of giving up hope.

We are not told exactly how Elijah heard and received the voice of God. Verse 14 reads like one of the oracles of the later prophets. A word or object (in this case Astarte's description of her empty bowl and jar in the larder) 'rings bells' in the prophet's mind. His faculty of 'second sight' or 'second hearing' resonates to Yahweh's message in response. It stirs inside him and bursts out in compressed, rhythmic form:

Jar of meal will not be spent,
jug of oil will not be emptied,
till I Yahweh send rain.

Perhaps the other messages came the same way. Perhaps Elijah heard a distinct voice in his head. Perhaps he saw a vision or dream of birds by the brook and a lone woman at Zarephath gate. Perhaps he met other people on his journey who advised him to go where he did, and Yahweh spoke through them. All these are ways he does speak; what matters is that Elijah heard. *We* have the inestimable advantage of God's complete book, where Elijah had only the early volumes. The Bible is the objective reference point to help us assess the genuine sound of every other 'word from the Lord'. In itself it contains everything we need to learn to serve God as Elijah did (2 Timothy 3:16–17). All Christian training should take the Bible as its basic text.

The chapter contains a remarkable string of miracles. (And they are recorded as real miracles, not as 'moral legends'. The rationalists have been at Elijah's mighty works, as they have at Jesus'. One attempt to 'explain away' the bowl and jar was to suggest that the widow's generosity in sharing her last crumbs shamed her better stocked neighbours into topping her up from their store-cupboards till the end of the drought. At the very least we must say that that is not the impression the author is trying to convey.) The striking thing in this account is that the miracles do not seize the headlines; they serve God's word. He speaks, and then they happen. 'I have commanded ravens, a widow . . .', 'The bowl, the jar will not run out . . .'. And, most impressive of all, when Elijah hands Hiram back to his mother alive, she does not say she now knows that Yahweh is the true God, or that he works wonders; but that he *really speaks through Elijah*. That is the punchline of the chapter. Clearly, even though it is not recorded, Elijah had received another promise from God, that her son would live again. Another triumph for the word of God!

God spoke. Elijah's part (and ours) is a four-fold response.

1. Wait and listen for God's word

He does not move from Cherith till God says go. As he entered Zarephath, you can see him feeling his way to hear God's confirming 'Yes, you've found the right widow.' He asks for a drink of water; she goes to fetch it. So far so good; but that is customary Eastern hospitality. He prods a little further: 'Please bring me some bread, too.' 'I swear that I haven't got any bread' sounds a firmly shut door. But there is a broad chink of light: she swears 'By the living Yahweh your God.' Then come the resonant bowl and jar, which draw out God's word of promise. Much bolder now, Elijah introduces the prophecy as from Yahweh *the God of Israel*. Most Sidonians would swear or jeer or pick up stones at such provocation. Astarte merely 'went and did as Elijah had told her'; God had shown him all right that she was the one.

2. Obey God's word

However crazy it may sound. Ravens! You will *not* find them in any directory of cordon bleu caterers. They don't even feed their own young. They are birds of prey, more used to stealing than giving. It seems more than a neat coincidence of the English language that they are spelt the same as 'ravenous' and 'ravening'. Yet, 'Elijah obeyed Yahweh's command.'

A widow with a sob-story: she already had another mouth to feed, and only one last meal to offer. She needed someone else to provide for her, not the other way round. But Elijah went in faith. Servants obey their master's command. You will never grow into Elijah, not even into the next intended stage of you, if you don't obey what God is telling you today.

3. Speak God's word

Elijah passed on God's message that came to him, and the chapter records how exactly it was fulfilled. 'As Yahweh had promised through Elijah, the bowl did not run out of flour nor did the jar run out of oil' (verse 16). And as we have seen, he must have given her some message of hope for her son's revival, so that she concludes, 'Now I know that the word of Yahweh in your mouth is truth.'

We are not all prophets or teachers. But we all have a responsibility to care for our fellow Christians and recommend the faith to outsiders. This often involves a word of encouragement, advice or good news. God gives his word to his servant to pass it on (Isaiah 50:4).

4. Live God's word

Astarte's final exclamation of discovery equates Elijah speaking God's word with his being 'a man of God', one who lives God's way. If we hear God's word, obey it and speak it, we are at the same time living by it and on it. The Bible becomes our food and fuel and life-blood. On this diet, God's will becomes the increasingly natural way to live.

I wrote this chapter in a Christian retreat centre on Mount Carmel (following Elijah's footsteps!). One of the volunteers working there feels called to concentrate on praying for Israel. She has printed a little motto-card for her friends:

Prayer Emphasis: that lives of believers in the land will so epitomize Elijah that Israel will speak

1 Kings 17:24: '. . . Now I know you are a man of God and that the word of the Lord from your mouth is truth.'

It would not be a bad prayer for yourself.

For further reflection

1. What are some of the lessons God has had to teach you since you have been his servant? Which have you found the hardest to learn? What do you think he is training you for at the moment?

2. What has been the most helpful thing you have learnt in or about prayer recently? What steps do you need to take to make sure that your 'prayer life' keeps growing?

3. How has God clearly spoken to you recently through his 'word'? What steps do you need to take to make sure that his word remains the driving force in your life?

Chapter three

The man who brought a nation to its knees

After some time, in the third year of the drought, the LORD said to Elijah, 'Go and present yourself to King Ahab, and I will send rain.' So Elijah started out.

The famine in Samaria was at its worst, so Ahab called in Obadiah, who was in charge of the palace. (Obadiah was a devout worshipper of the LORD, and when Jezebel was killing the LORD's prophets, Obadiah took a hundred of them, hid them in caves in two groups of fifty, and provided them with food and water.) Ahab said to Obadiah, 'Let us go and look at every spring and every river-bed in the land to see if we can find enough grass to keep the horses and mules alive. Maybe we won't have to kill any of our animals.' They agreed on which part of the land each one would explore, and set off in different directions.

As Obadiah was on his way, he suddenly met Elijah. He recognized him, bowed low before him, and asked, 'Is it really you, sir?'

'Yes, I'm Elijah,' he answered. 'Go and tell your master the king that I am here.'

Obadiah answered, 'What have I done that you

want to put me in danger of being killed by King Ahab? By the living LORD, *your God, I swear that the king has made a search for you in every country in the world. Whenever the ruler of a country reported that you were not in his country, Ahab would require that ruler to swear that you could not be found. And now you want me to go and tell him that you are here? What if the the spirit of the* LORD *carries you off to some unknown place as soon as I leave? Then, when I tell Ahab that you are here, and he can't find you, he will put me to death. Remember that I have been a devout worshipper of the* LORD *ever since I was a boy. Haven't you heard that when Jezebel was killing the prophets of the* LORD *I hid a hundred of them in caves, in two groups of fifty, and supplied them with food and water? So how can you order me to go and tell the king that you are here? He will kill me!'*

Elijah answered, 'By the LORD *Almighty, whom I serve, I promise that I will present myself to the king today.'*

So Obadiah went to King Ahab and told him, and Ahab set off to meet Elijah. When Ahab saw him, he said, 'So there you are – the worst trouble-maker in Israel!'

'I'm not the troublemaker,' Elijah answered. 'You are – you and your father. You are disobeying the LORD's *commands and worshipping the idols of Baal. Now order all the people of Israel to meet me at Mount Carmel. Bring along the 450 prophets of Baal and the 400 prophets of the goddess Asherah who are supported by Queen Jezebel.'*

So Ahab summoned all the Israelites and the prophets of Baal to meet at Mount Carmel. Elijah went up to the people and said, 'How much longer

will it take you to make up your minds? If the LORD
is God, worship him; but if Baal is God, worship
him!' But the people didn't say a word. Then Elijah
said, 'I am the only prophet of the LORD still left,
but there are 450 prophets of Baal. Bring two bulls;
let the prophets of Baal take one, kill it, cut it in
pieces and put it on the wood – but don't light the
fire. I will do the same with the other bull. Then let
the prophets of Baal pray to their god, and I will
pray to the LORD, and the one who answers by
sending fire – he is God.'

The people shouted their approval.

Then Elijah said to the prophets of Baal, 'Since
there are so many of you, you take a bull and
prepare it first. Pray to your god, but don't set fire
to the wood.'

They took the bull that was brought to them,
prepared it, and prayed to Baal until noon. They
shouted, 'Answer us, Baal!' and kept dancing round
the altar they had built. But no answer came.

At noon Elijah started making fun of them: 'Pray
louder! He is a god! Maybe he is day-dreaming or
relieving himself, or perhaps he's gone on a journey!
Or maybe he's sleeping, and you've got to wake
him up!' So the prophets prayed louder and cut
themselves with knives and daggers, according to
their ritual, until blood flowed. They kept on ranting
and raving until the middle of the afternoon; but no
answer came, not a sound was heard.

Then Elijah said to the people, 'Come closer to
me,' and they all gathered round him. He set about
repairing the altar of the LORD which had been torn
down. He took twelve stones, one for each of the
twelve tribes named after the sons of Jacob, the man
to whom the LORD had given the name Israel. With

these stones he rebuilt the altar for the worship of the LORD. He dug a trench round it, large enough to hold almost fourteen litres of water. Then he placed the wood on the altar, cut the bull in pieces, and laid it on the wood. He said, 'Fill four jars with water and pour it on the offering and the wood.' They did so, and he said, 'Do it again' – and they did. 'Do it once more,' he said – and they did. The water ran down round the altar and filled the trench.

At the hour of the afternoon sacrifice the prophet Elijah approached the altar and prayed, 'O LORD, the God of Abraham, Isaac, and Jacob, prove now that you are the God of Israel and that I am your servant and have done all this at your command. Answer me, LORD, answer me, so that this people will know that you, the LORD, are God, and that you are bringing them back to yourself.'

The LORD sent fire down, and it burnt up the sacrifice, the wood, and the stones, scorched the earth and dried up the water in the trench. When the people saw this, they threw themselves on the ground and exclaimed, 'The LORD is God; the LORD alone is God!'

Elijah ordered, 'Seize the prophets of Baal; don't let any of them get away!' The people seized then all, and Elijah led them down to the River Kishon and killed them.

Then Elijah said to King Ahab, 'Now, go and eat. I hear the roar of rain approaching.' While Ahab went to eat, Elijah climbed to the top of Mount Carmel, where he bowed down to the ground, with his head between his knees. He said to his servant, 'Go and look towards the sea.'

The servant went and returned, saying, 'I didn't see anything.' Seven times in all Elijah told him to

go and look. The seventh time he returned and said,
'I saw a little cloud no bigger than a man's hand,
coming up from the sea.'

Elijah ordered his servant. 'Go to King Ahab and
tell him to get into his chariot and go back home
before the rain stops him.'

In a little while the sky was covered with dark
clouds, the wind began to blow, and heavy rain
began to fall. (1 Kings 18:1–45a)

So then, confess your sins to one another and pray
for one another, so that you will be healed. The
prayer of a good person has a powerful effect. Elijah
was the same kind of person as we are. He prayed
earnestly that there would be no rain, and no rain
fell on the land for three and a half years. Once
again he prayed, and the sky poured out its rain and
the earth produced its crops.

My brothers, if one of you wanders away from
the truth and another one brings him back again,
remember this: whoever turns a sinner back from
his wrong way will save that sinner's soul from death
and bring about the forgiveness of many sins.
(James 5:16–20)

Ahab stood by the stables in his summer palace at
Jezreel. Several of the horses, and even some of the
mules, were sickening. It was the fourth summer of
the drought. Their feed had been reduced and reduced, till they were barely more than skin and bone.

'Steward,' he called.

Obadiah came running.

'Where are the stable boys? Why are they not
tending my sick horses?'

'One of them is too weak to work, Majesty. The other is helping in the kitchen where some of the cooks are off sick too.'

'I don't care about sick people. I want to save my animals.' Ahab thought of his army of 2,000 horses in Samaria, and shuddered at the idea of putting them down.

Obadiah wanted to scream at him, 'You stubborn fool. Why don't you turn back to Yahweh? You know he's promised rain if we give up this Baal-worship.' But he kept his steward's lips discreetly sealed.

'There's nothing else for it,' Ahab decided. 'We must find grass – every blade that's left. There's none round here. You and I must check every spring and stream in the land, in case there's any life left in them. You go north, I'll go south.'

They took two of the fitter horses and clattered out of the gate.

Obadiah felt faint as he forced the horse to stumble on. Nothing so far, but he had hopes of the river Kishon. He saw a figure approaching, but only as they drew level did it dawn on him who it was. He fell off the horse, and shook his head to make sure he was not hallucinating.

'Is it really you, sir?'

'Yes, it's me: Elijah. You can tell Ahab I'm here to meet him.'

'Have a heart, sir. He'll kill me. Don't you realize there's a price on your head? Where've you been all this time? And how do I know you won't do another of your disappearing acts the moment I've turned my back? If Ahab finds you're not here, he'll kill me on the spot. I've had enough of all this. I've done my bit. Don't have me killed, sir, please.'

He trembled like a leaf. He had good grounds to fear. They were at the foot of Mount Carmel; it's not a single peak, it's a range the size of a national park. It has over 2,000 caves in it. It would be the easiest thing for Elijah to dodge Ahab for another three and a half years.

'Don't worry,' said Elijah. 'I give my solemn oath on the living Yahweh, whom I serve, that I will stay here to confront Ahab today. Those are my orders from Yahweh.'

When Ahab arrived with a posse of soldiers in a cloud of dust and a thunder of hooves, he was snarling.

'So there you are – troublemaker! You're the most wanted man in Israel. I hope you're pleased with yourself and this famine you've brought down on us all.'

Elijah stayed calm. '*I'm* not the cause of all this trouble; *you* are. You incurred Yahweh's curse by breaking his laws and worshipping Baal instead. But now let's begin to put things right, shall we? Order all the people of Israel to meet me here at Mount Carmel.'

'All? Women and children?'

'As many as will come. The leaders of each tribe, at the very least.'

'Here on Carmel? This is the chief shrine of Baal, don't you know that? You're not thinking of coming over to Baal, are you?'

'Carmel will do well for what Yahweh has told me to do. And yes, bring those 850 prophets of Baal and Asherah that the queen keeps in her household.'

Ahab nodded, and turned his horses back to Jezreel. Only when he was 200 metres down the road did he realize what had happened.

'*He* gave orders to *me* – and I meekly did what he said! I came out here to arrest him and have him executed.'

He halted the soldiers and turned about. The solitary figure still stood there, imposing, commanding, daunting – like a crag of Carmel.

'Oh well,' thought Ahab, 'perhaps he can reverse the curse and stop the drought. That's the main thing.'

He yelled 'Turn again' to the soldiers and kicked his horse in irritation.

Mount Carmel

It is Elijah's great day. Most of his three-and-a-half-year training was preparing for this. We shall watch it through the eyes of those who were there, from dawn till dark.

The clash between the rival faiths and ideologies – Yahweh and Baal – finally comes to a head. Elijah's greatness was to focus the issues into one simple showdown. 'Simple' but massive, climactic, universal. Baal's resistance movement had rumbled on for 400 years, ever since the Israelites entered the land. Now a single pitched battle is to settle the matter.

The overwhelming victory on Carmel acted out on earth God's superiority over every opposing spiritual power. Baal's descendants live on in every anti-Christian force, faith and philosophy – from Jezebel's offspring of cruel totalitarianism and the ensnaring occult, to militant Islam and the West's most pervasive guiding spirit, materialism. We are caught in their permanent onslaught on Christianity. Our calling is to resist and fight back and take captives. We shall not win all in one day, as Elijah did. We do not live in a nation whose laws demand Yahweh-worship, as his did. But we can learn from his tactics and his weaponry. And I shall apply them in this chapter to one form of spiritual warfare open to us, evangelism. The parallels are not exact, but they are stimulating.

Make up your minds (verse 21)

It is early morning. The crowd has gathered. Elijah confronts them and, without any opening pleasantries, he challenges them. It is 'make up your mind' time. You've had long enough to sit on the fence and watch from the side-lines. You've got to jump – one way or the other. If Yahweh is God, go for him; if Baal, go for him. But whichever is God, he's for real; you can't play at it, you must worship. Throw in your lot, submit, belong, commit yourselves.

The stakes are high and Elijah has gone for broke. He is aiming for a national dedication to Yahweh, a renewal of the covenant, such as Samuel had staged (with thunder and rain) at Saul's coronation (1 Samuel 12); or, before that, Joshua at Shechem (Joshua 24); each in turn looking back to Moses' original sealing of the covenant on Mount Sinai (Exodus 24).

This is no bad opening gambit on our smaller platform, whether we are speaking evangelistically to a roomful or explaining Christianity to a friend or colleague. The gospel demands commitment, and we might as well make that clear from the start. God is king and calls us to surrender and be subject. Worship is submission of our whole lives. Becoming a Christian means making Jesus lord of my every activity, word and thought. Unless our conversation has this in view at least as a possible outcome, there is not much point in continuing it. Intellectual discussions without any intention of commitment are all very interesting, but ultimately a waste of time.

Jesus makes these all-or-nothing claims on us. If he turns out to be right, you must hand everything over to him. If you can prove him wrong, you don't have to give him another thought. Worship Baal instead. So which is it to be? How much longer will it take you to make up your mind?

But the people didn't say a word. Clearly it would take them a little longer than this. Some were probably confused (it *was* still the early morning!); others undecided one way or the other; some were for Yahweh, but afraid to make a public stand; others sided with the Baal prophets, but were unnerved by such a clear assault.

Our hearers too may be unready to make up their minds at once. Many have genuine questions or problems to clear away first. Many are simply unused to having to decide. The media still teach us that it is somehow smart to be agnostic, untied, free to criticize the different ways of life objectively. Fair enough. Give it time. So long as we are clear: you *will* have to make up your mind at 'the end of the day'.

The one who answers by sending fire (verses 22–24)
'OK then,' says Elijah. 'Let's open it up to a test. Two altars, two bulls; let's see which God can light

his own sacrificial fire. You can't say the dice are loaded in my favour – it's one against hundreds.' *That* broke the silence. 'Great idea. Let's have some action. Now we'll really see. In the red corner . . .'. The people shouted their approval.

Fire was an inspired choice. Not only was it the basic ingredient of public worship, where an animal was burnt to picture the people's devotion and make up for their sins. It was also a trademark of both deities: Baal the blazing sun-god; and Yahweh who had shown himself on Sinai in smoke and fire (Exodus 19:18), so that Moses described him as 'like a flaming fire' (Deuteronomy 4:24). He had sent fire to consume the sacrifice on the altar at least once before (1 Chronicles 21:26).

It might seem nice if we could conjure up a divine firework display today to prove God right and convince the sceptics. But signs to compel faith are not Jesus' usual way (Mark 8:11–12). Their use on this occasion was God's idea, not Elijah's; the prayer in verse 36 contains the revealing admission that 'I am your servant and have done all this at your command'. Miracles are God's initiative, not ours. In any case, a repeat performance would be to confuse the unique detail of Elijah's campaign (fire) with its repeatable outline (a fair comparison of faiths).

The point of Elijah's test is to discover the real God. 'The one who answers by sending fire – he is God.' Which religion is man-made, and which shows divine finger-prints? It is perfectly fair to stand the different beliefs people live by alongside each other and see how they compare. Christians don't need to be defensive about this. Many have resisted the 'comparative religion' approach in school RE syllabuses, wanting Christianity to have a privileged status. What are we afraid of? Provided the facts are fairly presented, provided Christianity has its fair turn among the others, it will make its own case. If, as we believe, it is the true religion of the true God, its truths will show up all the more clearly against the background of the false. We can relax, with Elijah. What if we are one in 850; perhaps the only one in over a thousand at our school or college or work-place? One plus God is the only statistic that matters.

Elijah compared the two faiths in public praise and prayer. That is a fair comparison still: what do Christians do on Sundays, Jews on Saturdays, Muslims on Fridays? What difference does it make to the way they live on Monday? In the New Testament burnt sacrifices have given way to the living sacrifices of believers' lives. Worship is not something I buy and give at the sanctuary; it is me. So it is fair, too, to compare the lives of famous Christians, famous Buddhists, famous Marxists. It is fair above all to compare the founders of the faiths, and their teachings, and their gods. How do Zeus or Brahma or Satan or the Reverend Moon stand up to Jesus? Come to that, how does alcohol or a fat pay packet or the latest pop idol stand up?

Pray to your god (verses 25–29)
Elijah is in sparkling form. His faith is bright and warm from Cherith, Zarephath and the days he has spent on the slopes of Carmel waiting for the tribes to gather. His vision of God is fresh, dynamic. 'You have first go,' he offers. 'Just one rule, remember – no firelighters, no cheating.' It was perhaps

nine o'clock in the morning.

The hundreds of prophets processed to Baal's high altar. They cut and dressed the starved and scrawny bull with utmost care. They prayed for fire. They shouted for it. They took it in turns, they yelled in chorus. They sang, they danced, they fell, they leapt. They formed in lines and circles and squares. But no answer came.

Often people need to reach the end of their own resources before they will turn to Christ. Only when they have pushed their own religion or *raison d'être* to the limits and found that it cannot support them, are they willing to give it up and look for something better. We may be too quick to press Jesus on them. As they face one of life's challenges – an exam, an interview, an illness, a broken relationship – we itch to say, 'Try praying to *my* God for help.' It may be better with Elijah to say, 'Pray to *your* God. How far does what you live for help you at your hour of need?' We may find it tragic or grotesque to watch, but some people will in no other way see the logical absurdity of how they are wasting their life.

At noon the sun reached its height, but it still hadn't kindled a twig. Some of the older and fatter prophets were conking out exhausted. Elijah was enjoying this. 'Oh no, you don't get out of it that easily. You're not shouting loud enough. Perhaps he's deaf or day-dreaming. Or I know, he must be on the loo: a bad attack of the runs, perhaps. Or he might be out at the moment. Or he's having a day off and he hasn't woken up yet. Come on, louder, louder!'

It is merciless. At Zarephath Elijah turned his sarcasm on God; here he uses it in God's cause. It is not necessarily unkind to the Baal-worshippers, because it is acute and true. It is the most effective put-down of pagan gods in all literature. This is precisely the point; they are just figments of human imagination, and so they have human weaknesses and limitations. Unlike Yahweh.

We have to stay with verse 27 a moment longer, because Elijah's jibes include 'Baal is a god!' Wooden, humourless scholars have concluded that Elijah's faith was only primitive and partial. He believed in Yahweh as Israel's god. But he clearly believed in Baal too, as the god of somewhere else to be kept in his proper place. How ridiculous! He's *joking*. Every step he takes on Carmel springs from total conviction that Yahweh alone is God, and that every other so-called god is an empty delusion. This was the simple faith of Israel, taught and written by Moses, to which Elijah was recalling the people. His humour shows all the more crushingly that Baal does not exist.

There can be a place for godly mockery in our evangelism. The role of comedy through the ages had been to puncture the false idols we take too seriously and show how absurd they are. It is a powerful gift to be able to expose the lunatic ideas that so many modern people swear by: the stars, touch wood, luck, fate, superstition.

The prophets of Baal weren't giving up yet. They struggled back to their feet and turned up the volume. They banged their drums and clashed their cymbals. They turned to their ritual for extreme cases. They flayed themselves with knives and daggers, till blood streamed down their faces and bodies. They cavorted and shrieked themselves into a state of near-hypnosis. Undoubtedly this was the full works, guaranteed to make Baal sit up and take notice. But it may have had another purpose along the lines of acting out the message to help him get the point. 'It's fire we need, Baal; you know, that red stuff, a big shoot of it out of the sky. *Now* please, like this!' And another vein was gashed.

All to no avail. By mid-afternoon, the prophets could croak and hop no more. They fell about on the ground, finished. As the Hebrew author so eloquently puts it, 'no voice, no answer, no attention was given them'. Baal had lost.

Yahweh sent fire (verses 30–39)
The people had long since lost interest. They were siding with Elijah now; they liked his jokes. 'Come over here and watch this,' he said; they gathered round.

He took them to a disused, dismantled altar of Yahweh. He picked up twelve of the stones that litter every hillside in Israel, and rebuilt the altar with them. 'Reuben, Simeon, Levi,' he began, naming a stone after every tribe. 'Issachar, Zebulun, Dan, Naphtali, Gad, Asher, and Joseph. He paused, then pointing at the top two pieces of rock, 'Judah and Benjamin'. The crowd gasped. How could anyone suggest that the southern kingdom belonged with the north? Most of the time they were at daggers drawn, if not actually locked in combat. Yet as they looked and talked together, Elijah's meaning became clear. He was calling them back to the God of their fathers; the God who had given them destiny, purpose and meaning as a united people.

We speak for Jesus against the shredded backcloth of a divided Christendom. Rival, disunited churches seem to cry out against the truth of what we are saying. We must admit that all is not well with the followers of Jesus. We ourselves are at fault and to blame. But a bad apple needn't mean the tree is diseased. We continue to point to the plan God has for human beings. He has displayed a perfect specimen in Jesus. He made us to depend on him, to interrelate with him in just the way that Jesus did. We have torn up the plan and hived off on our own; but he calls us to return, to rejoin his people, to learn to be at one with them and with him.

Elijah has got them on the edge of their seats. They watch his every move and they can see he's not cheating. Methodically, calmly, calling for help when he needs it, he digs a trench, places firewood on the altar, cuts the bull and lays it ready for sacrifice. Then he calls for water. Water! During the longest heatwave in memory! He fetches four two-litre jars and hands them round. 'Fill them.' There is a well, with a spring that never runs dry, but it's hundreds of metres down the hill. 'Fill them.' The four men set off and return after quarter of an hour, puffing and sweating. 'Pour them on the bull and the wood.' They do. 'Now fill them again.' He wants more water? Someone else have a go. And so again and again, till the sacrifice is drenched and the trench brimming with more standing water than anyone has seen for years.

What is he playing at? He's making Yahweh work all the harder. No ordinary fire would light the sticks now. But Yahweh is the God of the impossible. Let there be no doubt when the fire comes, that it comes from him. And when the rain comes after that, it will have Yahweh's stamp on it too. Elijah can afford to splash water around because the downpour is on its way to end the drought.

God chooses to make things difficult for himself. He could, if he wanted, convert people without any human intervention. Occasionally he does. But normally he gives us the treat and the delight of having a hand in bringing people back to God. That's the problem. We hash it, we bungle, we get in the way. We cannot do it on our own. God would do it so much better without us.

Yet in a wonderful way this uneven partnership brings pleasure and glory to God. 'We who have this spiritual treasure are like common clay pots, in order to show that the supreme power belongs to God.' (2 Corinthians 4:7). When people catch fire, in spite of us pouring cold water all over it, it can only be because God is at work. The encouragement is that, when it comes to evangelism, God *is* at work. 'When I arrived in Troas to preach the Good News about Christ, I found that the Lord had opened the way for the work there. . . . There is nothing in us that allows us to claim that we are capable of doing this work. The capacity we have comes from God; . . . God in his mercy has given us this work to do, and so we are not discouraged.' (2 Corinthians 2:12; 3:5; 4:1).

It is three o'clock – the time God commanded for afternoon sacrifice in the Jerusalem temple. Elijah walks to the altar and prays. No shouting or dancing or blood. Just a calm, quiet prayer of two sentences. 'Yahweh, do what you said. Prove you are God, so that the people of Israel know.'

And Yahweh sent fire. It was no lightning flash,

as some have suggested, because it fell from a cloudless sky. It was fire from above, not a man-made blaze from below; it burnt through sacrifice, wood, stones, earth, water from the top downwards. It was of intense, appalling heat; it burnt up the stones and evaporated the water. It scorched the earth and the people must have felt the blast. They threw themselves on the ground and called out the result: 'Yahweh is God; Yahweh is God!' They had made up their minds. Yahweh-worship in Israel was saved. Yahweh had won.

It was a stupendous victory. There is nothing else like it in the Bible. Except perhaps one other battle. Another sacrifice on another hill, also at three in the afternoon (Mark 15:34–37). Strangely, people expected Elijah to turn up then; but they'd missed the point. They also thought it was a defeat rather than a victory; there too they were deeply mistaken. The cross of Jesus was an overwhelming victory; it was *the* heavenly, spiritual triumph of which Carmel was just the carry-over. 'On that cross Christ stripped the spiritual rulers and authorities of their power' (Colossians 2:15). It is the one perfect sacrifice, acceptable to God, consecrating and making us acceptable at the same time. 'Because Jesus Christ did what God wanted him to do, we are all purified from sin by the offering that he made of his own body once and for all,' (Hebrews 10:10). It is the very centre of the Good News we aim to tell others. 'Our message is that God was making all mankind his friends through Christ. God did not keep an account of their sins, and he has given us the message which tells how he makes them his friends. . . . Christ was without sin, but for our sake God made him share our sin in order that in union with him we might share the righteousness of God,' (2 Corinthians 5:19,21). Time and again it is when we explain the cross that people finally yield to Christ. 'For God in his wisdom made it impossible for people to know him by means of their own wisdom. Instead, by means of the so-called "foolish" message we preach, God decided to save those who believe . . . we proclaim the crucified Christ . . .' (1 Corinthians 1:21,23).

Seize the prophets of Baal (verse 40)

Our cultured, tolerant ears don't like the sound of this grisly postscript to the battle. Modern re-tellings often gloss over it, particularly Elijah's part, implying that the people killed the prophets in an orgy of revenge for misleading them for so long. But the record is clear: Elijah gave the order; Elijah led the way down the hundreds of feet to the Kishon; Elijah killed them. At Muhraqa, the reputed site of the sacrifice on Carmel, there is a huge statue of Elijah with sword raised above a prophet cringeing under his foot. Presumably there were soldiers present who supplied the swords and perhaps helped Elijah to execute them. To be sure, the prophets were half-dead already, after their self-mutilation. But why did he need to finish them off?

Some have suggested that it was fair return for Jezebel's purge of Yahweh's prophets. But the real reason is that God commanded it. The law clearly requires that idolaters be put to death (Deuteronomy 13:12–18; 17:2–5). A few minutes ago the people re-committed themselves to Yahweh and his law. They can't now ignore it or flout it. Indeed, they would realize how lucky they were to get off free themselves; it was an act of mercy by Elijah to set the law only on the leaders, and not on all who had worshipped Baal.

We want to probe further. *Why* should God decree death for the idol-worshipper? Have you ever really understood God and how he feels? He made women and men as his most prized creation, unique on earth in being able to talk to him, know him and love him. They only flourish when they live with him; they wither and spoil when they turn away. They have a moral sense and know right from wrong. He has told them they must give account of their lives to him. How do you think he feels when they turn away, persist in turning away despite his open arms, and teach others to turn away? How do you think he feels when they flirt with other gods who hurt them and twist them and poison them; and then say they prefer it? How could he *not* stamp them out, to save the rest of the race? He has repeatedly warned that he will. In love and patience and hope he has held his hand so long that we begin to dream that it might never fall. But of course in the end it must.

These are solemn thoughts. And we shall need to include them in any full statement of the Christian faith to those who discuss it with us. It sometimes becomes clear that to one particular friend or group, we have nothing more to say. At the moment they are closed to the truths about Jesus. We want to part on good terms, so that they are open to later approaches when God's Spirit has prepared them further. We shall speak to them gently and lovingly. But it would not be fair to leave them without warning them that they face God's judgment unforgiven. This is the meaning of

Jesus' instruction to his mission teams: 'leave that place and shake the dust off your feet' (Matthew 10:14–15).

I hear the roar of rain (verses 41–45)

The day is not yet over for Elijah. As the sun sinks into early evening, we marvel at his supreme strength and fitness. The training in simple living and self-mastery have made their impact. He climbs back up to the top of the mountain. Ahab refreshes himself with a meal, but Elijah still has work to do. Baal is dead, the evil is cured, the rain should now return. But Elijah needs to pray; Yahweh told him, 'No rain or dew till you give the word'. Whether knowingly or not, Elijah sets to work to echo and apply Solomon's prayer of 100 years earlier:

> *When you hold back the rain because your people have sinned against you, and then when they repent . . ., humbly praying to you, listen to them in heaven. Forgive the sins of the King and of the people of Israel. Teach them to do what is right. Then, O Yahweh, send rain on this land of yours . . . (1 Kings 8:35–36).*

Prayer is the hardest work of all. It is Elijah's real *work*. It is the secret of his 'power'. It is the key to understanding this chapter.

Fleming James in his *Personalities of the Old Testament* says, 'No scene in the Bible brings absolute faith in prayer before us more vividly than

Elijah bowed down on the top of Carmel with his face between his knees.' Absolute faith in prayer. If we want to find God and see him at work, we must pray. If we want to see ground won in our dialoguing and duelling with other faiths, we must pray. There is no fruitful evangelism without hard work in prayer.

Elijah applies the lessons in prayer he learnt in Zarephath. He prays *alone*; though all of a sudden he has a servant in attendance. Perhaps some enthusiastic convert at the river volunteered; it may have been young Hiram himself – who knows? And Elijah *keeps praying*; not just three times as before, but seven times he sends the boy to look out towards the Mediterranean where the rain-clouds come from. At last a cloud appears, and as always, Carmel is the first of Israel's peaks to feel the rain.

And now there are further new blossoms on Elijah's praying. He is *sure that God will answer, because he is claiming God's promise*. God's word stood written: 'love Yahweh your God and serve him with all your heart. If you do, he will send rain on your land when it is needed' (Deuteronomy 11:13–14). When God has said something will happen, he inspires us not to sit around and twiddle our thumbs but to pray with greater faith than ever. What a boost to know that we are asking for something he wants to give anyway!

Elijah's prayer on Carmel exudes confidence and expectancy. 'I hear the roar of rain approaching,' he announces long before he can see it. This may be his prophet's 'second hearing', or it may be simple faith. He prays, and sends 'Hiram' at once to look for the answer. When it comes, he doesn't need the drops to start falling on his head before he is convinced; the merest pocket-size cloud is good enough for him.

In praying for others to become Christians, we can have this same certainty of God's collaboration. The Bible assures us that 'he does not want anyone to be destroyed, but wants all to turn away from their sins' (2 Peter 3:9). We pray from this firm foundation and look excitedly for the signs of change of heart. Mind you, people are a great deal more stubborn than rain-clouds; God respects their right to choose for themselves, and they may not yet be ready. But read on in your Bible for more promises and encouragements to pray with certainty.

The other new 'shape' to Elijah's prayer is his position – bowed down to the ground with head between his knees. He makes himself as small as he can. He is expressing *submission to God's control*. The commonest word for 'worship' in the Old Testament is literally this very idea, 'bowed down to the ground'. The essence of worship is not, as so many teach today, standing, clapping, raising arms, closing eyes or opening mouth, but rather prostration before God. It is the submission of captive to conqueror. It is the subject 'adoring' the king (literally, taking his hand or, as here, his foot to your mouth and kissing it).

This worship we supremely express in prayer. We say, 'Not my will but yours be done.' It is better that way; he knows best, his plan is perfect. He alone has the right and power to carry it through. There is nothing we on our own can do to put it into action. Who are we even to ask? We need him to move and do what he wants done. This is as true of our evangelistic activities as any others. We pray, 'your kingdom come, your will be done'.

As we pray for God's kingdom to advance, whether in major national revivals as at Carmel, or in our own little circle of friends, or the youth club we help to run, it is good to review all that Elijah learnt. Before invading Ahab's palace at Samaria, he prayed earnestly; at Zarephath he prayed alone, honestly, in concern and close identification with the person in need, with big vision and repeatedly; on Carmel he claimed God's promise and bowed to God's control. That sort of prayer is the way forward.

This is confirmed as we take a farewell look down the chapter from the top of Mount Carmel and across to its summary in James 5. The essence of the contest was 'let the prophets of Baal pray to their god, and I will pray to Yahweh' (verse 24). When he does pray to Yahweh his prayer breathes submission. The Baal prophets try to control God: 'Answer us because we are making such a noise; we've got the formula to make you do what we say.' Elijah lays himself open before God's control: 'Answer me so that this people will know that you, Yahweh, are God and that I am your servant.' His one desire is God's glory.

Or rather his *number one* desire. He has another longing – the reverse side of the first – that the people should return to Yahweh. His prayer ends in verse 37 with a most significant phrase: 'so that this people will know . . . *that you are bringing them back to yourself*'. The conversion has already begun. The people's prostration in worship two verses later is under active preparation by the Holy Spirit before they themselves realize it. How does

Elijah know? He's been praying for it all along. Certainly since he issued the Carmel invitation to Ahab, perhaps from long before. He prayed for the fire and for the people every bit as hard as he prayed for the rain. We look at our spiritually bankrupt, idolatrous countries and we weep. They need Elijahs to pray for them.

And James closes his letter by reminding us, 'Any one of you can be an Elijah.' Starting in the church fellowship where we pray for each other's spiritual health, he starkly highlights the powerful effect of prayer. Elijah prayed there would be no rain – and no rain fell for three and a half years. 'Once again he prayed' – the summary is so stark it would sound, if we did not know the reason, as though he had forgotten how to pray in the meantime. 'Once again he prayed, and the sky poured out its rain.' That is the power of prayer.

Now notice carefully where he turns our thoughts. As he signs off, what does he want us to use this powerful prayer for? 'My brothers, if one of you wanders away from the truth (like Israel) and another one brings him back again (like Elijah, by prayer and proclaiming the word of the Lord), remember this: whoever turns a sinner back from his wrong way will save that sinner's soul from death and bring about the forgiveness of many sins.' His focus is on evangelism, as ours has been in this chapter. Keep spreading the news about Jesus, and keep praying for it. Nothing could be more worthwhile.

For further reflection

1. Review 1 Kings 18. What comes across to you as the chapter's main message to the twentieth century church in general, and to you in particular? If evangelism is one possible application, what are others?

2. In this book we have applied 1 Kings 18 to evangelism. How easily do you find yourself discouraged in trying to help other people to become Christians? What encouragements from this chapter could help to rekindle you when zeal burns low?

3. Trace the theme of prayer through 1 Kings 18. Would you agree that 'It is the key to understanding this chapter'? Which facet of Elijah's praying most clearly 'speaks' to your present circumstances?

Chapter four

The man who wished he was dead

Elijah ordered his servant, 'Go to King Ahab and tell him to get into his chariot and go back home before the rain stops him.'

In a little while the sky was covered with dark clouds, the wind began to blow, and heavy rain began to fall. Ahab got into his chariot and started back to Jezreel. The power of the LORD came on Elijah; he fastened his clothes tight round his waist and ran ahead of Ahab all the way to Jezreel.

King Ahab told his wife Jezebel everything that Elijah had done and how he had put all the prophets of Baal to death. She sent a message to Elijah: 'May the gods strike me dead if by this time tomorrow I don't do the same thing to you that you did to the prophets.' Elijah was afraid, and fled for his life; he took his servant and went to Beersheba in Judah.

Leaving the servant there, Elijah walked a whole day into the wilderness. He stopped and sat down in the shade of a tree and wished he would die. 'It's too much, LORD,' he prayed. 'Take away my life; I might as well be dead!'

He lay down under the tree and fell asleep.

Suddenly an angel touched him and said, 'Wake up and eat.' He looked round, and saw a loaf of bread and a jar of water near his head. He ate and drank, and lay down again. The LORD's angel returned and woke him up a second time, saying, 'Get up and eat, or the journey will be too much for you.' Elijah got up, ate and drank, and the food gave him enough strength to walk forty days to Sinai, the holy mountain. There he went into a cave to spend the night.

Suddenly the LORD spoke to him, 'Elijah, what are you doing here?'

He answered, 'LORD God Almighty, I have always served you – you alone. But the people of Israel have broken their covenant with you, torn down your altars, and killed all your prophets. I am the only one left – and they are trying to kill me!'

'Go out and stand before me on top of the mountain,' the LORD said to him. Then the LORD passed by and sent a furious wind that split the hills and shattered the rocks – but the LORD was not in the wind. The wind stopped blowing, and then there was an earthquake – but the LORD was not in the earthquake. After the earthquake, there was a fire – but the LORD was not in the fire. And after the fire, there was the soft whisper of a voice.

When Elijah heard it, he covered his face with his cloak and went out and stood at the entrance of the cave. A voice said to him, 'Elijah, what are you doing here?'

He answered, 'LORD God Almighty, I have always served you – you alone. But the people of Israel have broken their covenant with you, torn down your altars, and killed all your prophets. I am the only one left – and they are trying to kill me.'

The Lord said, 'Return to the wilderness near Damascus, then enter the city and anoint Hazael as king of Syria; anoint Jehu son of Nimshi as king of Israel, and anoint Elisha son of Shaphat from Abel Meholah to succeed you as prophet. Anyone who escapes being put to death by Hazael will be killed by Jehu, and anyone who escapes Jehu will be killed by Elisha. Yet I will leave seven thousand people alive in Israel – all those who are loyal to me and have not bowed to Baal or kissed his idol.'

Elijah left and found Elisha ploughing with a team of oxen; there were eleven teams ahead of him, and he was ploughing with the last one. Elijah took off his cloak and put it on Elisha. Elisha then left his oxen, ran after Elijah and said, 'Let me kiss my father and mother good-bye, and then I will go with you.'

Elijah answered, 'All right, go back. I'm not stopping you!'

Then Elisha went to his team of oxen, killed them, and cooked the meat, using the yoke as fuel for the fire. He gave the meat to the people, and they ate it. Then he went and followed Elijah as his helper.
(1 Kings 18:44b – 19:21)

I ask, then: Did God reject his own people? Certainly not! I myself am an Israelite, a descendant of Abraham, a member of the tribe of Benjamin. God has not rejected his people, whom he chose from the beginning. You know what the scripture says in the passage where Elijah pleads with God against Israel: 'Lord, they have killed your prophets and torn down your altars: I am the only one left, and they are trying to kill me.' What answer did

God give him? 'I have kept for myself seven thousand men who have not worshipped the false god Baal.' It is the same way now: there is a small number left of those whom God has chosen because of his grace. (Romans 11:1 5)

Elijah's thoughts raced ahead into the future as mile followed mile. The prophets of Baal were dead and gone; Ahab would surely now instigate a thorough purge of worship through the land. He would sweep away Baal's shrines and restore the true praise of the God of Israel; he was bound to consult Elijah as Yahweh's proven mouthpiece. Elijah's feet pounded the rough track; but in imagination he was dancing on the grave of the religious decline of the last twenty years and more. With king and prophet reunited, an era of righteousness and peace lay ahead. The vision put wings on his feet.

He entered Jezreel and made straight for the palace. The journey is 17 miles, but his pace had never sagged. With God as his following wind, he had outstripped the king's chariot. And its driver was no slouch, as he forced the horses through mud and slush they had never met before. The royal cavalcade appeared at last. As they swished past, Elijah made out the huddled figure of Ahab. He whooped and sprang off again, dodging the chariot's spray. The palace gates opened; but the guards headed him off.

'The king will see me', he panted. 'Tell him I'm here.'

One of them retreated to the royal quarters. Elijah's teeth chattered in the sudden cold of the night; only now did he notice the rain, still teeming down. He untucked his cloak, but it was soaked through. When the rain comes to Israel, it is very thorough. He tried to shelter in the entrance to the guard-room; but they pushed him back.

At last the soldier returned.

'A message from the king?' asked Elijah.

'From the *queen*,' he replied. ' "Hear this, Elijah. You killed my prophets today. Tomorrow I shall kill you. May the gods strike me dead if I don't." '

The guards crowded in their barrack-room door. Now they'd see the sparks fly. This would be the knock-out blow to clinch the Carmel revolution. They could just hear Elijah's scorn as he sent Her High and Mightiness packing.

'By the living Lord I serve, it is Jezebel who shall die. This rain shall not stop pouring till her abominations are washed away, and she too is drowned in the Kishon.'

But the words never came. Elijah suddenly felt very empty, cold and old. The triumphs of this afternoon seemed years away. The God who had enveloped him in the blaze of noon had all at once disappeared in the dark. Elijah's faith, rock-like for so long, dissolved into sugar. He muttered indistinctly, and looked from face to face. He read suspicion, doubt, hostility, threat in their eyes, and he shrank visibly. He'd never noticed before that the human face can be frightening. He was on the brink of panic, when he spotted a familiar head – his servant. He must have arrived with the crowds from Carmel.

'Hiram,' he murmured in relief. 'Come along . . . something to do.'

The man and boy walked stiffly, self-consciously away into the dark. The soldiers looked at each other bewildered and shuffled back to their posts. The rain kept cascading.

Elijah was afraid

Elijah afraid? What had happened? His reserves had run very low. Years of devotion and austerity, of his one-man campaign against court corruption, had climaxed in the epic of Carmel. He had been God's lever to prise the nation back from its slide towards Baal. He had controlled a vast crowd. He had led the execution of nearly 1,000 men. He had prayed the heavens open. On top of this spiritual exertion he had run over half a marathon at record pace in driving rain. Barring the first Good Friday, it must have been the most draining day in history for a single human being. It took only the shock of Jezebel's retaliation to puncture him. But to Elijah it was a shattering shock. His victory was shallow, after all; the real root of the trouble, Queen Jezebel, had no intention of giving in.

'Up one minute, down the next' is a common phenomenon. Part of the reason is the old truth that pride leads to a fall. The Hebrew at the end of verse 4 probably means more than 'I might as well be dead'. The exact meaning is 'I am no better than my ancestors'. It is true enough that they *were* dead, and if Elijah is no more use than them, what is the point of living? This is indeed how depression can make us think. But surely the words also contain a glimmer of right self-perception. Events on Carmel have to some extent turned Elijah's head. He has come to see himself as 'Superman', saving the nation single-handed, succeeding where all previous generations had failed. Now he falls to earth with a bump: he has failed too. The whole revolution has failed, because evil is still enthroned and he ran away in fright. He has deserted his post, gone absent without leave. Superman is just a man after all. He is no better than his ancestors.

These collapses often occur just when things seem to have gone well. We are never so vulnerable as at the height of elation. Our faculties are at full stretch, and all too easily snap. If they have been consistently over-stretched, a fall is still more likely. Human resources are at best frail. And in the human life-cycle the onset of middle-age increases susceptibility to depression. Even God's strongest heroes remain human. We load them (and so encourage them to load themselves) with colossal expectations and responsibilities. The strain may be more than they can bear. Many have broken under it, and sustained permanent damage. Do pray for Christian leaders, especially those in the public eye.

Of course, it is not only 'big' and 'famous' Christians who break down as Elijah did. We all suffer pressure and disappointment; some manage to endure them, drawing steadily on God's comfort and stamina, but others of us miss our step and take an Elijah-size tumble. For Elijah fell a long way. His vision of God had been so intense that he had never before shown a moment's fear; but now he fled for his life. He had sought Ahab out to confront him with Yahweh's word; but at the mere report of Jezebel's threat, he bolted 100 miles to the border town of Beersheba. Even then he did not stop running. He trudged a further day into the desert, found a small shelter and dropped. He gave up, and asked to die. The prayer doesn't sound like an exaggeration; he'd left Hiram behind, presumably because he did not plan to return.

We all go through 'down' times, and it is perhaps some comfort to learn that even an Elijah is not exempt. We all, at different depths, experience waves of depression, usually triggered by some such shock or loss: failing a vital exam, leaving a happy home, losing a loved relative, hit by redundancy or physical handicap. We staked our all on *this* prayer; and God does not answer it as we had hoped. The feelings it unleashes echo the inner scream we yelled as babies when we thought ourselves deserted – I can't cope ('It's too much, Lord'); I'm all alone ('I am the only one left'); I'm no good ('I might as well be dead'); I'd like it all to end ('Take away my life'). Just underneath it lies the unspoken complaint: why have you allowed it to happen to me? It cries out for an answer. God begins his answer at once.

Elijah, what are you doing here?

Depression has been called the 'everyman' disease; mercifully, it need not be the 'always' disease. The story goes on to unfold how God treated (and still can treat) depression; and the lessons Elijah learnt through it.

Sleep and more sleep (verses 5–6)
Depression is not simply a spiritual or emotional state; it has physical causes too. Elijah was downright exhausted; and so are many of today's depressives. God's primary, natural cure is sleep, 'sore labour's bath, balm of hurt minds . . . chief nourisher in life's feast' (Shakespeare, *Macbeth*).

If you are under strain and stress, allow yourself more sleep. Rest will not come easily; you have to work for it! Plan your routine to ensure the hours in bed that you need. Catch up with a Saturday lie-in or Sunday afternoon snooze, or whatever suits your life-pattern. Cut out that surplus commitment or unhelpful late-night TV. And if your nights are interrupted by worry, bad dreams, wakeful children, seek appropriate help – medical, spiritual, practical or a blend; your sleep is too vital to be spoilt.

Ministering angels (verses 5–7)
It reads as if God put Elijah to sleep naturally, but had to wake him up supernaturally for lack of an alarm clock! It may be that the angel was invisible, at least the first time; verse 6 gives that impression. If Elijah showed no surprise, perhaps he was still half-asleep; or perhaps after Cherith's ravens, nothing surprised him any more. It *may* be that on the second occasion, the divine waiter turned out to be an Old Testament appearance of Jesus – the term 'Yahweh's angel' is used in that way elsewhere.

But the simple word 'angel' does not necessarily imply an apparition from heaven. 'Angel' means no more than agent or messenger; we *may* be reading here of an early 'Good Samaritan', a kindly traveller whose practical concern for Elijah fitted into God's purposes. His provision for our needs is often miraculous more in the timing and placing (a day's journey into the desert), than in the means he uses.

Maybe, perhaps; perhaps, maybe; we can't be sure exactly what happened. Either way, the important point is universal. When we are down and out, he knows the help we need, and he gets it to us . . . *somehow*. When we're miserable, even a dog wagging its tail or a child offering a drawing seems an angel of mercy.

Food and drink in plenty (verses 5–8)
It was probably at least three days since Elijah had eaten; that was stretching things, even for his disciplined body. Much nervous exhaustion today is worsened by bad or inadequate eating. A morning's work on nothing but coffee . . . nibbles in the office instead of a proper lunch-break . . . junk food gobbled on the run . . . this kind of diet saps energy and weakens resistance.

The meal God spread for Elijah was basic in the extreme; but it restored him, and fortified him for a mammoth trek through the desert. 'Forty days' may be a symbolic rather than literal number, meaning 'a long time'; the journey was about 200 miles and should not have taken *so* long (unless he lost his way). But it was still a formidable achievement on such slight and simple fare, even if the second meal was more substantial than a loaf of bread. If we want our bodies to last the course and give God the best possible service, we need to work out the food they need and eat it; neither skimping nor stuffing ourselves. It helps digestion to make meal-breaks a real break, switching our minds off work. Francis Bacon gave this wise advice: 'To be free-minded and cheerfully disposed at hours of meat . . . is one of the best precepts of long lasting.'

Something to do (verses 7–8)
Depression inclines the sufferer to sit around and mope; he or she feels useless. It is vital to have some definite activity to engage us: God sent Elijah on a journey. Action, movement, a task (however simple), all help to refresh the body, occupy the mind and lift the spirits. They can also be a safe way to release frustration. In a time of depression and anger, I worked out my aggression on my bike pedals as I rode to work each day. This is one advantage of regular exercise, whether walking the dog, jogging, tennis, a work-out in the gym or a swim in the sea. Elijah's route-march had medical and psychological value as well as the spiritual motive we shall uncover in a moment.

We are not clearly told whether Elijah knew where he was making for when he set off, nor whether he knew how long the trip would take. But it seems likely; it would be rather hard of the angel to say the journey might be too much for him, without giving any travel directions. It is a big help when we are emotionally vulnerable to have clear targets to aim at for each day, each week. To begin with, they should be small and easily manageable so that we regain confidence and a sense of achievement. Perhaps the walk *did* take Elijah 40 days after all, if in his weakened state he could only cope with a short burst each day.

Time (verse 8)
It is, as we have just seen, an open question whether the walk took the full forty or a mere ten to fourteen days. Whichever, it allowed time to elapse; and time is one of God's great healers.

When I was depressed, a wise friend told me, 'You will get better, but you must give it time.' Someone who is depressed cannot possibly 'snap out of it' or 'pull themselves together' instantaneously. They need the pressure taken right off, so that they feel no-one is pushing or chivvying them. They must have time to absorb the shock and come to terms with it. Time to learn the lessons from it. Time to re-build. Progress will be sure, but slow.

Back to square one (verses 8–9)
With a homing instinct for where he would find God, or at the command of the Lord's angel, Elijah retreated to Mount Sinai. This was where the Israelite religion first took full shape, when God gave Moses the Ten Commandments and hundreds of other regulations (Exodus 19–34). The Hebrew of verse 9 says Elijah went into *the* cave; this may have been the exact 'opening in the rock' where Moses saw God pass by (Exodus 33:22).

Low periods are a God-given opportunity to get back to fundamentals. Very likely it was our drifting from them that contributed to the breakdown. The Christian equivalent of Sinai is Calvary, where Jesus sealed the new covenant with his blood. Returning to ask and find his full and fresh forgiveness is often the first step back on to our feet. Or you may need to retrace the route to your own Christian starting-place. When did it all begin for you? Did you get things right then? If so, where have things gone wrong since? What do you need to do to repair the damage?

A chance to talk it out (verse 9–10,13–14)
A depressed person is usually a hubbub of conflicting voices and emotions inside. He or she desperately needs to release the thoughts and feelings to someone who will listen. So God asks Elijah the question that opens the floodgates. And often one outlet is not enough. When God repeats the question, Elijah comes out with the identical complaint; that shows how deeply it had swollen and festered inside him.

The words of verses 10 and 14 repay close study. They are the authentic tones of the over-wrought: self-justification ('I have always served you'); indignation at the injustice of everyone else ('they have broken their covenant . . .'); self-pity ('I am the only one left'); exaggeration of the problems ('*they* are trying to kill me' – after all, it was only Jezebel. He is accusing 'the people of Israel'; but even if he had good reason to suspect that their repentance was disappointingly superficial, they weren't trying to kill *him*. The last time he'd seen them, they were killing Baal's prophets.). Under the words lies a deep anger with God for allowing such unfair treatment of his servant.

When you feel this sort of resentment, don't cork it up till you explode. Tell God what's on your chest; he's quite big enough to take it. Or if you find that difficult, pray and look for a Christian friend who will listen without shock.

A new revelation (verses 11–13)
We are peeling our way steadily deeper into God's dealings with a wounded soldier. The enigmatic truth is that when we are in the dark we often see God more clearly than in the light. God shows himself to those who know their need of him, even if they hardly dare look. Elijah only stepped out on to the proffered viewing point after Yahweh had passed by; and even then he covered his face in awe and a right sense of unworthiness.

Despite all this, he grasped a vital new insight. The Lord put on a mighty wind, an earthquake, a fire – enough to re-shape the landscape permanently. This was the traditional Old Testament language God spoke when he appeared in person (Judges 5:4–5). It was the way he had shown himself on Sinai to Moses (Exodus 19:18). It was a very 'Elijah-type' method of making his presence felt. The name Elijah uses in verse 10 is more pointed than 'LORD God Almighty'; he calls him 'Yahweh sabaoth', the Lord of hosts, commander of armies. He sees God as the mighty, crusading warrior. Less than a week ago he had invoked Yahweh as 'the one who answers by sending fire'. So now it was not just the hills and rocks standing on their heads; it seemed to be God as well. The devastating new revelation was that *he was not in the fire*.

He came now to Elijah in 'the soft whisper of a voice'. The Hebrew can be translated even more delicately: 'the sound of gentle silence'. To be sure, God is king enough to display signs and wonders, and judge enough to underline his demands in thunder; he does command unbeatable armies. But there is always more to God than even his most experienced servants have understood. He also loves us enough to be with us all the time – in silence as well as in activity. He can make the earth move all right, but more often he whispers to our inmost being. Earth-shattering revivals like Carmel come once in a life-time, if that; God's soft voice can come everyday. He teaches a way of enduring and winning that can be gentle as well as strong; his power does not always have to be punching the enemy on the jaw. If we are always out frantically chasing the lightning, we miss what God is saying to us in his still, small voice. This is the danger of the spiritually hyper-active, the workaholic, the 'Western' temperament that must be forever achieving bigger and better results. God is not in the hustle and panic and storm, so much as in the profound calm he can bring us at the heart of stormy circumstances.

This was probably a new perception for the Old Testament as a whole. David had perhaps glimpsed it in some of his psalms; but now God says it himself. In his love he chose Elijah to receive the revelation – and not the all-conquering Elijah of 1 Kings 18, but the down-and-out Elijah of chapter 19.

A large part of the cure for depression is to be quiet and still in God's presence. Spend time consciously listening to him, praying, reading the Bible and other books that will help you reset your sights on him. It takes effort to shut out all the other noises in our lives that would drown 'the soft whisper of God's voice'. It takes time and dedication to learn to hear 'the sound of gentle silence'. But when we do, God makes himself known to us in the way that specially fits *us*. Elijah was beginning to learn that he was himself. God had made him unique for a unique calling. He did not have to struggle to be a carbon copy of Moses.

A new role (verses 15–16)
Another blessing of a burn-out or mid-life crisis such as Elijah went through is that it forces us to take stock of our hopes and dreams; it makes us reassess whether we are spending our limited reserves of time and energy on what we really want to be and become. The result is often a realignment of priorities; or, as here, a new sense of God's call and direction. *God* will never make us redundant or condemn us to the scrap-heap (even if human employers sometimes take this convenient way out). He does not prolong our sick leave, but wants to send us back to work refreshed. But he may well change and develop what we have seen as *our* ministry, our preserve, our little corner of influence. So Elijah is to move over from his role as Yahweh's lone ranger. He has borne the glare of the limelight long enough. He is now to anoint and appoint the next generation of star players on the world stage.

If depression or a breakdown leads to a change of job, we should try not to view it as a failure. It is an opportunity to find ourselves afresh, to rediscover the zest in living. Elijah didn't act the rejected first fiddle. He took to his switch from performer to producer so readily that he seems to have majored on just one of the main tasks in his new job description: coaching the next prophet Elisha. For in fact it was Elisha who in due course proclaimed Hazael king and oversaw the anointing of Jehu (2 Kings 8:7–15; 9:1–13). In many jobs there comes a stage when we transfer from being a full-time front-line practitioner, and invest our experience in training others to replace us and go beyond us. The same applies for positions of responsibility in church or Christian Union. It is happy and healthy to recognize the right moment through mature judgment; sadly (but not disastrously), many of us only reach it by running ourselves to a standstill, like Elijah.

Assistance (verses 19–21)

It had never been quite fair to say 'I am the only one left'. Elijah had been an isolated prophet, certainly, but 'Hiram' had stayed with Elijah through his nightmare flight. Still, Elijah needed more than a servant; he needed a helper. A kindred spirit who would understand and share his vision, pray with him, work with him, complement his strengths and weaknesses. Someone he could not just dismiss when he wanted to give up. Someone who would give the companionship and affection that most people find in husband or wife – it is significant that when God moves Elijah on to 'higher service', Elisha laments him as 'My father!' (2 Kings 2:12). For too long Elijah had soldiered on without fellowship.

An insistence on keeping the whole of life to ourselves can lead to depression. And depression can open our eyes to the value of human friendship. Good friends are one of life's best safeguards for health and happiness. When I was depressed, my counsellor's 'prescription' was to work at the close relationships I had neglected, to build a personal support system. And the experience of running aground on my own made me consider for the first time whether God wanted me to get married. I judged that in my case he did, though of course loneliness on its own is a poor foundation for a marriage; there need to be other reasons as well, principally a positive sense of belonging to each other.

Vindication (verse 17)
Only after meeting many other personal needs, God turns to answer Elijah's implied accusation of verses 10,14. No, God will not ignore the covenant-breakers forever; he holds back his punishment in mercy, but eventually it will fall. Yes, Elijah is right to be outraged at the gravity of what they have done. It is every bit as serious as he always said. The dynasty of Omri and Ahab will be over-thrown, and the process is about to start.

The roots of depression often include an injured sense of not being listened to and not receiving the credit due to us. Few things are as desolate as feeling slighted and misunderstood. God is careful to reassure his servant here before sifting out the less justified part of his complaint.

Correction (verse 18)
Human perceptions and emotions are never wholly right. Elijah has been so taken up with his lone stand for righteousness, that he never noticed (or he discounts) the sizeable army who could have stood with him. On Carmel he was rather enjoying, perhaps priding himself on, this wrong idea that he was Yahweh's only champion (18:22). He has got things out of proportion, and part of his cure will be to learn to take a more balanced and accurate view.

And another of his complaints in verse 10 is stronger than Good News Bible's 'I have always served you – you alone'. His precise words were, 'I have been very jealous for Yahweh of armies.' Jealousy is a difficult emotion to keep pure. Only God can hold it for long in sin-free balance. This is the right sort of jealousy – jealous *for* God; but it so easily goes sour into the wrong sort – being jealous *of* anyone else who claims to serve him, and still more of those who *don't* serve him but get away with it.

So long as we stubbornly insist that we were fully in the right, our healing and growth are stunted. Only by submitting to God's clearer estimate of the facts, and admitting that we were wrong, can we move forward. God's correction comes as a relief, and it is usually such good news. 7,000 – probably another symbolic number for a larger total still – have resisted the lure to corruption! It is not as many as Elijah had hoped for in his unrealistic view of Carmel's victory, but it is far more than he had feared in his despair.

Again God chooses Elijah's depression, in fact Elijah's wrongheadedness, as the moment to reveal another new truth. In times of persecution, even as fierce as Jezebel's, God preserves a loyal remnant of followers to carry out his purposes. Again and again through the Bible's history this 'small number left' hang on against the odds and God's plan survives intact. Noah and family survived the flood; Lot escaped from Sodom; Zerubbabel's Jews returned from exile. In Romans 11 Paul quotes this revelation to Elijah as the moment when the doctrine of the 'remnant' was first formuated. We shall come back to it; when we look on a wider canvas than Elijah's personal biography (and its comfort for a depressed Christian today), the New Testament points to this verse 18 as the key to the chapter.

Elijah left

So Elijah emerged from another furnace – in very different shape from Zarephath, which was the first. What has really happened? Some feel that he is fully restored; refined for a new, background ministry among the 7,000. Others feel that he failed the ultimate test; by clinging unrepentantly to his self-righteousness in verse 14, he missed the chance of leading the whole people into a genuine reformation.

There is probably truth in both accounts. The quiet helper in the youth club is wonderfully reclaimed from the drug addict he was last year. But he is way short of the brilliant concert pianist he was training to be when he picked up the drug habit. Or is he? Perhaps the youth leader is a rounder, wiser, happier person than ever the pianist would have been. Perhaps Elijah, who used to court and cultivate the style of the solo genius, got stuck in a rut of going it alone. Could he find deeper fulfilment in forsaking the role of superstar and forming a team instead? We shall see.

For further reflection

1. Do you regard depression in Christians as an illness/handicap (equivalent to malaria or a broken leg), or a spiritual failing, or something else? In any 'down' periods you have experienced, have you felt as depressed as Elijah in this chapter/less so/ more so? Have you discovered any helpful ways to handle your low feelings? How conscious have you been of God's help at such times?

2. What would be your personal 'square one' of bedrock certainty that you would return to, if your Christian faith seemed about to collapse? And who do you look on as your personal 'support system', the friends with shoulders to cry on when needed?

3. How does the 'doctrine of the remnant' – God working through the faithful few, as illustrated in verse 18 and taught in Romans 11:1–5 – encourage you at the moment?

Chapter five

The man who condemned three kings to death

1. Ahab

Near King Ahab's palace in Jezreel there was a vineyard owned by a man named Naboth. One day Ahab said to Naboth, 'Let me have your vineyard; it is close to my palace, and I want to use the land for a vegetable garden. I will give you a better vineyard for it, or, if you prefer, I will pay you a fair price.'

'I inherited this vineyard from my ancestors,' Naboth replied. 'The LORD forbid that I should let you have it!'

Ahab went home, depressed and angry over what Naboth had said to him. He lay down on his bed, facing the wall, and would not eat. His wife Jezebel went to him and asked, 'Why are you so depressed? Why won't you eat?'

He answered, 'Because of what Naboth said to me. I offered to buy his vineyard, or, if he preferred, to give him another one for it, but he told me that I couldn't have it!'

'Well, are you the king or aren't you?' Jezebel

replied. 'Get out of bed, cheer up and eat. I will get you Naboth's vineyard!'

Then she wrote some letters, signed them with Ahab's name, sealed them with his seal, and sent them to the officials and leading citizens of Jezreel. The letters said: 'Proclaim a day of fasting, call the people together, and give Naboth the place of honour. Get a couple of scoundrels to accuse him to his face of cursing God and the king. Then take him out of the city and stone him to death.'

The officials and leading citizens of Jezreel did what Jezebel had commanded. They proclaimed a day of fasting, called the people together, and gave Naboth the place of honour. The two scoundrels publicly accused him of cursing God and the king, and so he was taken outside the city and stoned to death. The message was sent to Jezebel: 'Naboth has been put to death.'

As soon as Jezebel received the message, she said to Ahab, 'Naboth is dead. Now go and take possession of the vineyard which he refused to sell to you.' At once Ahab went to the vineyard to take possession of it.

Then the LORD said to Elijah, the prophet from Tishbe, 'Go to King Ahab of Samaria. You will find him in Naboth's vineyard, about to take possession of it. Tell him that I, the LORD, say to him, "After murdering the man, are you taking over his property as well?" Tell him that this is what I say: "In the very place that the dogs licked up Naboth's blood they will lick up your blood!" '

When Ahab saw Elijah, he said, 'Have you caught up with me, my enemy?' 'Yes, I have,' Elijah answered. 'You have devoted yourself completely to doing what is wrong in the LORD's sight. So the

*L*ORD *says to you, "I will bring disaster on you. I will do away with you and get rid of every male in your family, young and old alike. Your family will become like the family of King Jeroboam son of Nebat and like the family of King Baasha son of Ahijah, because you have stirred up my anger by leading Israel into sin." And concerning Jezebel, the* LORD *says that dogs will eat her body in the city of Jezreel. Any of your relatives who die in the city will be eaten by dogs, and any who die in the open country will be eaten by vultures.'*

When Elijah finished speaking, Ahab tore his clothes, took them off, and put on sackcloth. He refused food, slept in the sackcloth, and went about gloomy and depressed.

The LORD *said to the prophet Elijah, 'Have you noticed how Ahab has humbled himself before me? Since he has done this, I will not bring disaster on him during his lifetime; it will be during his son's lifetime that I will bring disaster on Ahab's family.'*
(1 Kings 21:1–24, 27–29)

Ahab smiled with unfriendly eyes. 'Let me have it. I want it. Lovely leeks it would grow.'

'No,' said Naboth, 'I can't.'

'I'll find you a bigger one, a better one. I'll pay.' That's it, he thought; everyone has his price.

Naboth was horrified. 'But that would break Yahweh's law.'

'Oh, you and your Yahweh. Always Yahweh, Yahweh, Yahweh getting in my way.' Ahab stamped back to the palace in a huff.

He flung himself on his bed. The servants called

him to lunch; he turned his back on them without a word. They brought the food to his chamber: no answer. His Majesty was sulking.

Her Majesty came to enquire. She knew the way round his bad moods. 'Poor diddums, tell Jezebel what's the matter.'

'Naboth won't let me buy his vineyard, waaah!'

'Huh, so this is how you play the king in Israel. I'll show you how to do it properly. Clever Jezebel will get diddums his lovely vineyard.'

Long pause. Perhaps if somebody *else* broke Yahweh's law . . . Ahab turned over and smiled.

Jezebel sat at Ahab's desk. She pressed his seal on the papyrus documents she had addressed to the members of the town council. '*That* should do it,' she smiled. 'They only need two witnesses.'

A good afternoon's work. Four crimes at a sitting: forging the king's signature, calling a bogus festival, false accusation and 'judicial' assassination. All, of course, with a fifth one in mind: illegal possession of the vineyard. Tee-hee.

The council jumped to it. The vineyard 'fell vacant'. The queen smiled. The king smiled. He leapt on a horse and trotted out to survey his new property. It was delightful, everything he wanted. . . .

He jumped out of his skin. His blood turned to ice. It was as if an arrow had shot him through.

'Elijah,' he gasped. 'How did you find out?'

I will do away with you

God is our judge. He watches what we do. It may

seem for sixteen verses that he is nowhere around, but he sees. Everything we do is 'in Yahweh's sight' (verse 20).

He does not often step in and interrupt the human world he has put us in. He waits in the hope that people will come to their senses and mend their ways. But he warns and reminds and accuses. People may try to stifle their consciences, their knowledge of what he calls right and wrong. But sooner or later he sends Elijah to pronounce judgment. Today he sends you and me, his church.

It is not easy. It is frightening. Ahab and Jezebel behave like spoilt children in this chapter, but their power is terrifying. The last time Elijah spoke to Ahab, he ran away in panic. Now God digs him out of retirement and sends him back. The message is even worse to announce – last time it was 'Here beginneth the rain'; now it is 'Here endeth your reign.' That took courage.

We too shall need courage to announce God's judgment to secular authorities who overstep the mark. But there are times when we must do it. When they sin, they make God angry. This chapter of the biography will be an anatomy of God's anger. And in his anger he sends his prophets to rebuke and condemn. The Bible shows scene after scene where God's servants confront national rulers with his word of judgment.

Not that we shall often meet presidents or prime ministers. But they are not the only abusers of power. Sin is the natural bent in everyone, and every human institution tends to drift towards injustice unless constantly checked and controlled. We shall meet misunderstanding, prejudice, inhuman procedures, wrong decisions even in

people and organizations with the best of motives
and most of whose work is honourable. Police, law-
courts, doctors, hospital authorities, management
in public services, our own boss or elected
representatives or church leaders – all at times
make mistakes. The mistakes often have bad results
and make others suffer. When we see others suffer,
God certainly wants us to do more than moan and
mutter. He may want us to do more than
sympathize and comfort, good though that is. He
may want us to take up their case and complain;
not simply as our democratic duty, but as our
witness (tacit or explicit) to the God of justice. The
indignation we feel is an echo of his.

God's anger and judgment are not uncivilized
or unworthy. They are a compliment to human
responsibility. Today Ahab would probably plead
that he couldn't help himself; 'When Jezebel comes
on strong, your honour, she reminds me of my
mother and I just can't say no.' God knows when
he is being hoodwinked. He pronounces sentence
on Jezebel *and* Ahab; they are both adult human
beings, accountable for their actions.

His judgment is scrupulously fair. It exactly fits
the crime: you threw Naboth to the dogs; very
well, they will now eat you. You took Naboth's
inheritance; so now you will lose your own.
Further, Ahab 'devoted himself completely to
doing what is wrong' (verse 20). The world is literally 'sold' himself, a vivid contemporary image. A
citizen could pay his debts by selling himself into
slavery. Ahab had, as it were, done away with
Yahweh's ownership by selling his soul to evil; 'Fair
enough,' says Yahweh, 'I will do away with you.'
The sentence has to go beyond just Ahab and

Jezebel, because a king's actions carry greater weight than a private individual's. He represents his royal family and influences his subjects. So Ahab's dynasty must come to an end.

Furthermore, God's judgments come true. He means what he says. Within three years Ahab was dead (1 Kings 22:37–38), completely if not quite geographically fulfilling the poetic curse of verse 19. Twelve years later Jezebel died exactly how and where God said (2 Kings 9:36–37). Ahab's remaining 70 descendants soon followed her (2 Kings 10:10). The agent of God's judgment was Jehu, just as God had told Elijah in advance (1 Kings 19:16–17).

The possible site of the palace at Jezreel is today a ruin, under excavation. Next to it, perhaps on the site of Naboth's vineyard, is a kibbutz, a farm growing fruit and vegetables. God's judgments are awesomely pure.

Haratzachta vegam yarashta?

No, that is not a misprint. It is the Hebrew of the first half of verse 19, rendered into our alphabet. Try saying it aloud. It is much more clipped, rhythmical, throaty and menacing than 'After murdering the man, are you taking over his property as well?' More like 'So you're a con man as well as a cut-throat.' In Israel it has become a haunting proverb to express God's horror at sharp practice.

It is a new note in Elijah's prophecy. Till now he has condemned Ahab's affront to God in worshipping Baal; here he tackles Ahab's crime against his fellow-man in killing and robbing Naboth. The theologians sum up the message of the Old Testament prophets as 'ethical monotheism'. 'Monotheism' means there is only one God; that God, they insisted, was Yahweh. Now we meet their 'ethical' demand: Yahweh's desire is social justice, loving neighbour as well as God. He knows no separation between religion and politics.

Naboth stands for the politically oppressed and downtrodden in every age, including in horrific measure our own. Ahab and Jezebel stand for the unchecked, tyrannical use of power by rulers who come to regard opponents as inconvenient insects to crush underfoot. In the world as he has made it, God seldom cushions the ride for his followers; he does not deflect the bullet aimed at Christians, or hold back the torturer's lash. Naboth died a martyr for his heroic stand; so did his sons (2 Kings 9:26), presumably to prevent any tiresome claims to inheritance.

God allows it to happen; but it stirs up his anger. It defies his law, coded in detail for Israel in the Old Testament, but also planted in the conscience of every human being. Naboth's vineyard was protected by law. It belonged to God (Leviticus 25:23–24) and to Naboth's family (Numbers 36:7); it was not Naboth's to sell. He was one of the 7,000 who revered Yahweh's word. Not even the government had the right to take it from him (Ezekiel 46:18). God had legislated that no king can ever be 'above the law' (Deuteronomy 17:18–20).

In his anger God sends prophets to apply the law and its consequences. When his blood boils, theirs boils too. *'Haratzachta vegam yarashta?* I will bring disaster on you.' Where we see people denied their rights, we too must protest and fight for them and declare God's verdict in any way open to us – even when the offender is the head of state. We need not be lone Elijahs. Groups of Christians, or churches, can achieve a great deal when they speak and act together.

Not during his lifetime

Ahab came to heel (verse 27). It sounds a fairly self-centred repentance; he has been 'gloomy and depressed' at Yahweh's rebuke before (20:43; 21:4) and it led to no improvement then. But this time it took resolution to fast and wear sackcloth before the court and especially Jezebel; he even went to bed in sackcloth! It was good enough for God.

'Have you noticed how Ahab has humbled himself before me?' he asks Elijah (verse 29). His quick-eyed love detects the first signs of repentance and runs out to meet it. Even when it is partial and grudging, he rewards it. The death sentence on Ahab's dynasty must stand, but Yahweh postpones it to allow Ahab the dignity of being the first to go. And unlike Jezebel, he at least received royal burial (1 Kings 22:37,40).

It is important for us to be true to God's heart, which even in anger longs for reconciliation and the chance to forgive. 'Do you think I enjoy seeing an evil man die?' asks the Sovereign Yahweh. 'No, I would rather see him repent and live' (Ezekiel 18:23). We too must rejoice and give thanks when he does.

2. Ahaziah

In the seventeenth year of the reign of King Jehoshaphat of Judah, Ahaziah son of Ahab became king of Israel, and he ruled in Samaria for two years. He sinned against the LORD, following the wicked example of his father Ahab, his mother Jezebel, and King Jeroboam, who had led Israel into sin. He worshipped and served Baal, and like his father before him, he aroused the anger of the LORD, the God of Israel.

After the death of King Ahab of Israel, the country of Moab rebelled against Israel.

King Ahaziah of Israel fell off the balcony on the roof of his palace in Samaria and was seriously injured. So he sent some messengers to consult Baalzebub, the god of the Philistine city of Ekron, in order to find out whether or not he would recover. But an angel of the LORD commanded Elijah, the prophet from Tishbe, to go and meet the messengers of King Ahaziah and ask them, 'Why are you going to consult Baalzebub, the god of Ekron? Is it because you think there is no god in Israel? Tell the king that the LORD says, "You will not recover from your injuries; you will die!" '

Elijah did as the LORD commanded, and the messengers returned to the king. 'Why have you come back?' he asked.

They answered, 'We were met by a man who told us to come back and tell you that the LORD says to you, "Why are you sending messengers to consult Baalzebub, the god of Ekron? Is it because you think there is no god in Israel? You will not recover from your injuries; you will die!" '

'What did the man look like?' the king asked.

'He was wearing a cloak made of animal skins, tied with a leather belt,' they answered.

'It's Elijah!' the king exclaimed.

Then he sent an officer with fifty men to get Elijah. The officer found him sitting on a hill and said to him, 'Man of God, the king orders you to come down.'

'If I am a man of God,' Elijah answered, 'may fire come down from heaven and kill you and your men!' At once fire came down and killed the officer and his men.

The king sent another officer with fifty men, who went up and said to Elijah, 'Man of God, the king orders you to come down at once!'

'If I am a man of God,' Elijah answered, 'may fire come down from heaven and kill you and your men!' At once the fire of God came down and killed the officer and his men.

Once more the king sent an officer with fifty men. He went up the hill, fell on his knees in front of Elijah, and pleaded, 'Man of God, be merciful to me and my men. Spare our lives! The two other officers and their men were killed by fire from heaven; but please be merciful to me!'

The angel the LORD said to Elijah, 'Go down with him, and don't be afraid.' So Elijah went with the officer to the king and said to him, 'This is what the LORD says: "Because you sent messengers to consult Baalzebub, the god of Ekron – as if there were no god in Israel to consult – you will not get well; you will die!" '

Ahaziah died, as the LORD *had said through Elijah.* (1 Kings 22:51 – 2 Kings 1:17a)

As if there were no god in Israel to consult

Jezebel had made a thorough job of her son Ahaziah. He worshipped and served Baal wholeheartedly. None of the early warning signs of Yahweh's anger brought him to his senses. The empire put together by David and Solomon began to crack up, as Moab rebelled and broke away. Then Ahaziah fell off the roof and lay seriously injured.

Still his first thought was of Baal. He sent to the Philistine Baal for a prognosis. This Baal-zebub was the insect-god – the name means 'lord of the flies'; perhaps swarms were infesting and infecting Ahaziah's wounds. Baalzebub's shrine at Ekron was a noted centre for fortune-tellers.

Once again Yahweh calls out his ultimate weapon, Elijah. He supplies the answer to the king's question, 'You will not recover from your injuries.' And he announces it as the judgment on his sin: 'Because you sent messengers to consult Baal-zebub, you will die!' God's feeling of bewilderment and pain can be heard in the refrain, sounded three times, 'Is it because you think there is no god in Israel?' (verses 3,6,16).

We do not begin to understand God's anger (or, come to that, the story of Elijah, or the Old Testament, or Christianity itself) till we see that God is jealous. That was how he described himself when he introduced the Ten Commandments (Exodus

20:5, where the Good News version translates 'I am Yahweh your God and I *tolerate no rivals*'). When the law is repeated in Exodus 34, he makes it even more explicit, 'Jealous' is my middle name, he says in effect ('Do not worship any other god, for Yahweh, whose name is Jealous, is a jealous God', verse 14, NIV). The idea disturbs us because we think of jealousy as a sin. In human beings it usually is. As we have seen, it turned sour even in Elijah. But in God jealousy is a natural and healthy state of mind; it is pure and perfect. It means passionate concern for someone's best interests. He is jealous *for* us his creatures, because he knows what is for our good. He only becomes jealous *of* (angry and resentful towards) other gods when he sees us wasting the energy and love he gave us on ideas, passions, things that will harm and belittle us. This will need explaining as we proclaim God's anger.

Ahaziah sent to Baalzebub. How could he, how dared he? He knew the truth well enough. Even if Jezebel had kept him away from Mount Carmel, he knew that his father had died early after coming under Yahweh's curse. He was under the same curse himself. But he chose to resist it.

It is four years since the Naboth incident. The spectral Elijah has suddenly cropped up again to haunt the family conscience; at a greater distance this time, but instantly recognizable (verses 7–8). Ahab repented, but not Ahaziah. He sends out a troop of soldiers to 'get Elijah'.

May fire come down from heaven and kill you!

This incident causes more trouble to our twentieth century ideas than any other in Elijah's life. Some dismiss it as typical of 'the God of the Old Testament' – savage, primitive, unchristian. They point out that Jesus rebutted the suggestion that he should 'do an Elijah' (Luke 9:54–55). Others think that Elijah with his special powers has become trigger-happy, mowing down his enemies with a heavenly flame-gun. These are understandable reactions, but the thinking is sloppy. We may wish this part of the story wasn't there, but it is. Indeed the fire from heaven receives three-fold emphasis (verses 10,12,14), just as the other expression of God's jealousy did.

At the time everyone clearly understood that it was *God's* fire, not Elijah's. It was fire 'from heaven'. It was announced in the punning, 'word-association', rhythmic form of a God-given prophetic oracle: 'If I am a man (Hebrew *iesh*) of God, let fire (*eesh*) of God come.' If that had been a false, man-made prophecy, the answer would have been silence. But instantly the fire came, showing that God had breathed and spoken.

We feel sorry for the 'innocent' soldiers. They were just obeying orders; surely Ahaziah was the guilty party. But in the clash of faiths there are no neutrals. If they had been sympathetic to Yahweh, they could have approached as Obadiah did before Carmel, or as the third officer did here. The contrast with the third officer suggests that the first two aligned themselves with Ahaziah's bloodthirsty defiance. 'We know you call yourself the man of

Yahweh, but we've come to get you for the king.' They are part of his repeated, almost mindless opposition to Yahweh's clear warning. The new generation were behaving as if Carmel had never happened.

Some people interpret this fire from heaven as a virtual repeat of Mount Carmel: 'I'm still Yahweh and I'm still here'. This is close, but there is an important difference. The fire on Carmel was ferociously hot to burn stones, as we have seen; but no-one was hurt. Elijah stood next to the altar; the altar was consumed in a blazing flash, but Elijah was not burnt. This is a picture of God's fire when we are in the right relationship with him. As with all the Old Testament burnt offerings, it symbolizes a life given over to serving him. It makes us think of other peaks of God's history when he showed himself in fire that flamed but did no harm: the call of Moses at the burning bush (Exodus 3:2), and the descent of the Holy Spirit on the Day of Pentecost (Acts 2:3).

On this hill on the way to Ekron, however, the fire kills. This is God's fire of judgment, let loose on those who attack him. He had unleashed it before, when people rebelled against him during the desert wanderings (Numbers 11:1–3; 16:35). It is a foretaste of the fire of final judgment which Jesus and the New Testament teach as the fate of evil-doers (Matthew 13:40–42; 2 Thessalonians 1:7–8; Revelation 20:11–15). It is the fate that all rotten things deserve; soiled rags go in the incinerator. The wonder is not that God burst out in literally blazing anger in 2 Kings 1; rather that he does not do so more often, and to us all. Every act of sin, let alone an assassination threat on his prophet, kindles God's anger. The glory of the age we live in is that God withholds his judgment, to give us time to get right with him. That was why Jesus told James and John not to think of calling down fire from heaven.

The profound truth is that God *is* fire (Hebrews 12:28–29). Any fire will either warm us or burn us, depending where we stand. If we 'worship God in a way that will please him, with reverence and awe', his fire will consecrate us and set us alight. If we choose to reject his love, his fire will destroy us. Everyone will fall into God's fire one day, and experience it as anger or as acceptance, as destruction or dedication. The choice is ours. This terrifying responsibility given to human beings should spur us on to warn people how real God's anger is. We urge them to make peace with him now. We never now when lightning may strike.

3. Jehoram

Jehoram son of King Jehoshaphat of Judah had six brothers: Azariah, Jehiel, Zechariah, Azariahu, Michael, and Shephatiah. Their father gave them large amounts of gold, silver, and other valuable possessions, and placed each one in charge of one of the fortified cities of Judah. But because Jehoram was the eldest, Jehoshaphat made him his successor. When Jehoram was in firm control of the kingdom, he had all his brothers killed, and also some Israelite officials.

Jehoram became king at the age of thirty-two, and

he ruled in Jerusalem for eight years. He followed the wicked example of King Ahab and the other kings of Israel, because he had married one of Ahab's daughters. He sinned against the LORD, but the LORD was not willing to destroy the dynasty of David, because he had made a covenant with David and promised that his descendants would always continue to rule.

During Jehoram's reign Edom revolted against Judah and became an independent kingdom. So Jehoram and his officers set out with chariots and invaded Edom. There the Edomite army surrounded them, but during the night they managed to break out and escape. Edom has been independent of Judah ever since. During this same period, the city of Libnah also revolted, because Jehoram had abandoned the LORD, the God of his ancestors. He even built pagan places of worship in the Judaean highlands and led the people of Judah and Jerusalem to sin against the LORD.

The prophet Elijah sent Jehoram a letter, which read as follows: 'The LORD, the God of your ancestor David, condemns you, because you did not follow the example of your father, King Jehoshaphat, or that of your grandfather, King Asa. Instead, you have followed the example of the kings of Israel and have led the people of Judah and Jerusalem into being unfaithful to God, just as Ahab and his successors led Israel into unfaithfulness. You even murdered your brothers, who were better men than you are. As a result, the LORD will severely punish your people, your children, and your wives, and will destroy your possessions. You yourself will suffer a painful disease of the intestines that will grow worse day by day.'

Some Philistines and Arabs lived near where some Sudanese had settled along the coast. The LORD incited them to go to war against Jehoram. They invaded Judah, looted the royal palace, and carried off as prisoners all the king's wives and sons except Ahaziah, his youngest son.

Then after all this, the LORD brought on the king a painful disease of the intestines. For almost two years it grew steadily worse until finally the king died in agony. His subjects did not light a bonfire in mourning for him as had been done for his ancestors.

Jehoram had become king at the age of thirty-two and had ruled in Jerusalem for eight years. Nobody was sorry when he died. They buried him in David's City, but not in the royal tombs. (2 Chronicles 21:2–20)

Yahweh condemns you

The names of the kings of Israel and Judah are a sore trial. This Jehoram is not to be confused with the other Jehoram (his brother-in-law) who was king of Israel at the same time! *This* Jehoram was king of Judah, the southern kingdom. As Elijah continues the purge of Ahab's family, we see him now move on from his son to his son-in-law. For Jehoram had married Athaliah, a true daughter of Jezebel. She inherited her mother's authority. The Chronicler's verdict is that, despite Jehoram's godly upbringing by his father, 'he followed the wicked example of King Ahab *because* he had married one of Ahab's daughters' (my italics).

There is one difference in the outcome. Because this is Judah, David's descendants are still on the throne, and God has promised not to obliterate the line (verse 7). Otherwise the story has a depressing sameness with the other two. He repeats the double sin of Ahab: building pagan places of worship and murdering those who stood in his way. He ignores the same warning signs God had sent to Ahaziah: parts of the empire break off. As Steve Turner puts it in one of his pungent poems:

History repeats itself.
Has to.
No-one listens.

It is time to call for the old trouble-shooter. This time, partly perhaps because it is the other kingdom where he has not worked. Elijah sends the message in a letter. This is one of the most helpful methods for us too. We do not often get the chance to speak face to face to a senior government official, especially of another country. But we can put our complaints in writing. And not only to the oppressor direct. Letters to the press, to an MP, to interested pressure groups, are all good channels for spreading God's word and calling to action. Letters to the radio are reckoned to represent the views of 1,000 people each; they are taken seriously. Where there has been sin, we shall need to explain why it is offensive and what a better course of action would be; however we phrase it, the impact of our message must include 'The Lord condemns'.

Nobody was sorry when he died

Somehow this bleak little non-epitaph in verse 20 has the opposite effect to what its words say. When Jehoram died under God's judgment, nobody mourned him or even honoured him with a royal grave. Presumably the writer agreed that it was good riddance and not worth spilling a tear over. Yet there is something very moving, deeply tragic, about the son of good King Jehoshaphat wasting away through a terminal disease into the nothingness of a virtual 'unperson'. To be sure, *God* was sorry that he died this way. Our proclamation of his anger will be tempered by his sadness at the tragic waste of so much human potential in the carnage of sin.

A single chapter, one tiny half-country, a short eight-year reign – yet we read of fratricide, judicial murder, persistent warfare, armed invasion, idolatry; all rebounding on the king so that his palace is looted, his family deported, his health seeping away in a humiliating, painful illness. Whether through the Bible or the TV news, God calls his people to weep over a world so wildly adrift and to pray for national leaders who will rule in righteousness. Then we shall not need all this negative criticism and complaint. We shall be able to congratulate and give praise.

It's Elijah!

Three kings set themselves up to blow a raspberry

125

at God. They worshipped soul-destroyingly, they ruled unjustly. Three times God launched his sin-seeking missile, Elijah. It was recognizably the Elijah of old: fearless, uncompromising, shot through with God's anger and jealousy, setting us a matchless example of how to denounce sin and awaken a careless world to God's judgment.

End of story? Many commentators reckon that, apart from his final journey into heaven, these are the parting glimpses we have into his life. They picture him living alone in the mists of Carmel, unseen for years at a time, except when called by God's word or angel to sally forth on a mission of judgment. For the rest, there are long gaps of silence which the Bible account does not fill in for us.

This is true as far as it goes. But there are puzzles about what Elijah says and does in these three incidents which prompt us to ask questions and to wonder whether the gaps are quite as silent as they seem. The questions dangle from the end of the chapters, tantalizingly unanswered.

The first question is, could Elijah really have done so little? 1 Kings 17–19 give us a comparatively full picture of three and a half years in his life. Admittedly they show only nine days from that period in any detail. But they give a clear impression of a fast mover, full of initiative (at God's prompting), alert with energy and dash, a creative thinker, taking action to save his country. By contrast, the three chapters in Kings and Chronicles we are now looking at cover at least ten years, perhaps as many as fifteen. They record only three outings; and, significantly, in all that time Elijah fails to carry out two of the three tasks God gave him at Sinai: anointing Hazael and Jehu. We could conclude that Carmel knocked the stuffing out of him and he never recovered to live at the old pace. But that doesn't fit the Elijah we see in Naboth's vineyard; the old boldness, timing, sarcasm, authority are back, the old tough grasp of the issues, knowledge of the court personnel, ability to think quickly and express God's judgment in short, piercing dagger-thrusts.

And yet that doesn't quite fit either. It's not just the old Elijah; there are new developments in him as well. At the vineyard we hear him for the first time voice God's concern for social justice; and he appears to learn God's merciful response to Ahab's repentance 'on the job'. It is as if Elijah is back in training college again; 1 Kings 21:28–29 sound exactly like a tutor or senior consultant teaching his apprentice. So our second question is, what was this further in-service training in new insights preparing him for?

Then we come back to the puzzling business of the fire from heaven. Having said all we can about *God's* jealousy, we still stumble over Elijah's apparent jealousy for his own position: 'If *I* am a man of God, may fire come down and kill you!' We have seen him concerned for his position before – 'prove that I am your servant', 'they are trying to kill me!'; but at his best he has been far more absorbed in God's position – 'In the name of Yahweh, whom I serve', 'prove that you are the God of Israel'. So why does he now sit on his dignity?

The fourth and biggest puzzle surrounds Elijah's letter to Jehoram. One question is where did Elijah get his detailed knowledge of events in the southern kingdom? But the really thorny problem is that it looks as if Elijah was no longer alive – on earth! – when he wrote it. And there is no indication that we are talking about a posthumous letter inspired by a 'dead' spirit! Jehoram ruled in Jerusalem for eight years after Jehoshaphat; but Jehoshaphat is still alive in 2 Kings 3 when he consults Elisha after Elijah's death. One explanation is that Elijah's letter was prophetic in the sense that it foresaw the events it describes before they happened. There is nothing to prevent God doing this, but it sounds unlikely here. For one thing, all Elijah's other condemnations respond to sins already committed. For another, unless the letter carried a 'Not to be opened for ten years' sticker, it would make odd reading for Jehoram before he had done the things he was accused of; it might even have the perverse effect of putting them into his mind.

A large part of the problem drops away with an understanding of Judah's customs for succeeding to the throne, and with a careful reading of the chapter in Chronicles. As King David neared his death, it was still unknown who would succeed him. Adonijah the eldest surviving son tried to stage a coup; to counter this, David authorized Solomon's immediate coronation. For however long David lived on, there were in effect two kings of Judah in tandem (1 Kings 1,2). They thus set a precedent of overlapping co-regency, which several later kings copied, including Jehoshaphat and Jehoram, as the lengths of reign recorded in Kings and Chronicles can demonstrate. Jehoram became co-regent with his father while Ahaziah was king in Israel, in other words while Elijah was still alive. In the Chronicles account this is clearly the moment referred to in verse 3: 'because Jehoram was the eldest (son), Jehoshophat made him his successor'.

Then comes verse 4, 'When Jehoram was in firm control of the kingdom' – not yet sole king, but joint-king with his father who at least twice left the country on military expeditions – 'he had all his brothers killed, and also some Israelite officials.' (The 'Israelite' officials are thoroughly confusing, but they probably did not belong to the northern kingdom of Israel. They may have been 'friendly' but over-officious advisers from the neighbouring court; but the author of Chronicles writes from the perspective of the southern kingdom and more than once calls Judah 'Israel', because he regards it as the *true* Israel, the faithful part of the once united kingdom.) There was no need for Jehoram to fear his brothers and the officials trying to take the throne from him, as he was 'in firm control'. The more likely reason for killing them would seem to be that they opposed and criticized his policy of favouring his wife's Baal-worship.

Only then do we reach verse 5, 'Jehoram became king at the age of thirty-two, and he ruled in Jerusalem for eight years', the usual formula for becoming the one and only king. It is clear that his murders and idolatry – the sins condemned in Elijah's letter – had already come to light in Elijah's lifetime.

Elijah may have sent the letter then and there – if so, it had a long time-fuse, as Jehoram did not contract his terminal illness for at least six years. If, however, the events in 2 Chronicles 21 are in correct historical sequence, the letter – although *written* earlier – was not delivered till after the 'promotion' of Elijah himself. If this is a correct reconstruction, we are left with our fourth question, who posted the letter?

These questions push us into the next chapter.

For further reflection

1. What is your own reaction to the heavy emphasis in these stories on God's anger, justice and condemnation? How would you explain this portrayal of God to someone who believes that it conflicts with the Bible's teaching about God's love?

2. Have you ever felt moved to complain, protest or campaign as a Christian? What effect did it have? What hope can we have of halting unjust or tyrannical regimes in the world today? How can we bear positive witness to the Christian Good News while appearing to be negative and critical?

3. Who is the 'Naboth' God wants you to stand up for?

Chapter six

The man who set a fashion with just one suit of clothes

The L*ord* *said, 'Return to the wilderness near Damascus, then enter the city and anoint Hazael as king of Syria; anoint Jehu son of Nimshi as king of Israel, and anoint Elisha son of Shaphat from Abel Meholah to succeed you as prophet. Anyone who escapes being put to death by Hazael will be killed by Jehu, and anyone who escapes Jehu will be killed by Elisha. Yet I will leave seven thousand people alive in Israel – all those who are loyal to me and have not bowed to Baal or kissed his idol.'*

Elijah left and found Elisha ploughing with a team of oxen: there were eleven teams ahead of him, and he was ploughing with the last one. Elijah took off his cloak and put it on Elisha. Elisha then left his oxen, ran after Elijah, and said, 'Let me kiss my father and mother good-bye, and then I will go with you.'

Elijah answered, 'All right, go back. I'm not stopping you!'

Then Elisha went to his team of oxen, killed them, and cooked the meat, using the yoke as fuel for the fire. He gave the meat to the people, and they ate it.

Then he went and followed Elijah as his helper.
(1 Kings 19:15–21)

The time came for the LORD *to take Elijah up to heaven in a whirlwind. Elijah and Elisha set out from Gilgal, and on the way Elijah said to Elisha, 'Now stay here; the* LORD *has ordered me to go to Bethel.'*

But Elisha answered, 'I swear by my loyalty to the living LORD *and to you that I will not leave you.' So they went on to Bethel.*

A group of prophets who lived there went to Elisha and asked him, 'Do you know that the LORD *is going to take your master away from you today?'*

'Yes I know,' Elisha answered. 'But let's not talk about it.'

Then Elijah said to Elisha, 'Now stay here; the LORD *has ordered me to go to Jericho.'*

But Elisha answered, 'I swear by my loyalty to the living LORD *and to you that I will not leave you.' So they went on to Jericho.*

A group of prophets who lived there went to Elisha and asked him, 'Do you know that the LORD *is going to take your master away from you today?'*

'Yes, I know,' Elisha answered. 'But let's not talk about it.'

Then Elijah said to Elisha, 'Now stay here; the LORD *has ordered me to go to the River Jordan.'*

But Elisha answered, 'I swear by my loyalty to the living LORD *and to you that I will not leave you.' So they went on, and fifty of the prophets followed them to the Jordan. Elijah and Elisha stopped by the river, and the fifty prophets stood a short distance away. Then Elijah took off his cloak, rolled it up, and struck the water with it; the water divided, and he and Elisha crossed to the other side on dry ground. There, Elijah said to Elisha, 'Tell me what you want me to do for you before I am taken away.'*

'Let me receive the share of your power that will make me your successor,' Elisha answered.

'That is a difficult request to grant,' Elijah replied. 'But you will receive it if you see me as I am being taken away from you; if you don't see me, you won't receive it.'

They kept talking as they walked on; then suddenly a chariot of fire pulled by horses of fire came between them, and Elijah was taken up to heaven by a whirlwind. Elisha saw it and cried out to Elijah, 'My father, my father! Mighty defender of Israel! You are gone!' And he never saw Elijah again.

In grief Elisha tore his cloak in two. Then he picked up Elijah's cloak that had fallen from him, and went back and stood on the bank of the Jordan. He struck the water with Elijah's cloak, and said, 'Where is the LORD, the God of Elijah?' Then he struck the water again, and it divided, and he walked over to the other side. The fifty prophets from Jericho saw him and said, 'The power of Elijah is on Elisha!' They went to meet him, bowed down before him, and said, 'There are fifty of us here, all strong men. Let us go and look for your master.'
(2 Kings 2:1–16a)

This chapter unfolds a thesis to answer the questions at the end of the last one.

Could Elijah really have done so little during his last ten to fifteen years on earth? I suggest that, far from brooding alone on Mount Carmel, he was busy training a new generation of prophets. This 'retirement ministry', spread over ten or more years, was just as strategic as that earlier day on Carmel; and in its quite different way, just as demanding. My suggestion that during these years he advanced from the age of 43 to 55 is only a guess. But he was certainly not very old. Each 'leg' of the farewell journey in 2 Kings 2 (Gilgal to Bethel to Jericho) is about 14 miles by crow's flight; the foot-route is a great deal longer as it twists up through mountain passes. To cover it in a single day (verses 3, 5) requires supreme fitness, especially if, as verse 11 implies, they walked it rather than riding donkeys.

What was God equipping Elijah for as he gave him new in-service training? Partly, of course, he was helping Elijah to keep growing and developing in character; he does this with all of us. When he retreated to Mount Sinai, Elijah had become rather 'stuck'. As he is healed and 're-made', God asks him three times to do familiar work. But it is not simply back to the old routine, repeating Samaria and Carmel; each assignment contains new dimensions and challenges.

If, as I shall try to show in this chapter, Elijah's *main* work through these years was to live among new prophets and teach them, two of these new dimensions come at once to light. The Ahab, Ahaziah and Jehoram missions needed the experience and presence of Elijah as 'front man'; but he would come as the representative of a growing prophetic community, giving him new identity and security. And the lessons God taught him as he went would be to benefit the trainee prophets, not just Elijah.

So, as he strikes Ahaziah's soldiers down, why does Elijah make so much of his status? 'If I am a *man of God*, may fire come down . . .' Perhaps because he sees a new future for men of God, and is helping to build it himself. His concern is less for himself than for the calling and honour of other prophets.

And who delivered the letter to Jehoram? Probably Elisha, as Elijah's successor. The 2 Kings account of Jehoram's reign is sandwiched amidst the stories of Elisha's life. If Elisha did not take the letter in person, it would have been some of the young prophets under his guidance. Together they formed a network of prophetic communities, with communication between them (*e.g.* 2 Kings 5:22), by which news would flow of events in the court of Judah. These communities became the seed-bed of prophecy's revival.

The evidence for all this at first sight looks slender; but on investigation it is clear and compelling. Some of my reconstruction has to be speculation, but it rests on strong pillars.

Each previous chapter in the biography – Samaria, Cherith, Zarephath, Carmel, Sinai, and condemning the three kings – has shown us Elijah as the solo operator, the archetypal 'one-man minister'. It is highly significant that our last, lingering view of him, in 2 Kings 2, shows him now collaborating with Elisha and a group of prophets.

Elisha

The simple retort to the 'lone prophet in the clouds'

view of Elijah is that he did *not* live alone during this period of his life. Elisha was constantly with him. 'He went and followed Elijah as his helper' (1 Kings 19:21). 'He was Elijah's assistant' (2 Kings 3:11). The other prophets all call Elijah his 'master' (2 Kings 2:3,5,16). When Elijah tried to be alone, Elisha refused time and again to leave him (2 Kings 2:2,4,6)! Whether he accompanied the Naboth and Ahaziah missions, we do not know; but if Elijah did undertake them alone, that was abnormal by his post-Sinai practice. The norm is 1 Kings 19:21: Elijah and Elisha together. The two passages at the head of this chapter show us how they met and how they parted. Both reveal Elisha as more of a companion than the mere 'servant' of 18:43–44 and 19:3.

Elijah's attendant
When Elijah took off his cloak and put it on him, Elisha understood the symbolic action as a call to full-time service. He left home; he burnt his yoke and oxen and offered himself to God and to Elijah on the sacrifice of his old means of livelihood. Elijah's typically clipped, terse utterance in 19:20 (literally 'Go back. What have I done to you?') is probably somewhere in between Good News Bible's two attempts to explain it. It contains the relaxed good nature of the main text's 'All right, go back. I'm not stopping you'; but it also contains, and goes beyond, the magnetic appeal of the footnote, 'Go on, but come back, because what I have just done to you is important.' It is in fact a characteristically pregnant Hebrew pun. 'What have I done to you?' means 'Think over its meaning, work it out. When you have, you'll realize that it's not

really *my* action that counts. I was simply passing on to you Yahweh's call. He wants you to follow me. And of course he allows time to say good-bye.'

Following Elijah was a sacred duty Elisha meant to see through to the end. His refusal to leave his post is out of loyalty to the living Yahweh – and to Elijah himself (2 Kings 2:2,4,6).

Elijah's pupil
'They kept talking' (2:11): there's another pregnant phrase, surely an understatement this time. The passage unavoidably brings to mind Jesus' forty days with the disciples after the resurrection. *He* aware that he would soon be taken from them, anxious to teach them all they could take in and more; *they* nervous at the challenges ahead, knowing they needed the master's own spirit to guide them. So here; only the time was shorter still.

When Elisha is left alone, he learns fast that Yahweh the *God* of Elijah, and not Elijah himself, is the source of the inspiration and power he needs (verse 14). There is a wobbly moment, a possible false start, as he seems to rely on Elijah's cloak and all it stands for. But he learns at once from the mistake, if mistake it was, and strikes the water again.

Crossing the Jordan was not the only of Elijah's miracles Elisha learnt to reproduce. He must often have heard his teacher speak of the 'bottomless' oil-jar and the widow's son in Zarephath. Two of his earliest love-deeds were to follow in the wake of these, the second almost as if from the text-book (2 Kings 4). So faithfully did he trace his master's steps that his own epitaph exactly echoed Elijah's (13:14).

Part of Elijah's training was to delegate some of his own commissions to Elisha. God had told him to anoint Hazael as king of Syria and Jehu as king of Israel. His pupil took over the responsibility. And as part of the lesson he in turn learnt the art of delegation! Although he met Hazael himself (2 Kings 8:9–13), he sent one of his own pupils to Jehu (9:1–3).

Elijah's son

When Elijah 'passed on', Elisha tore his cloak in two. This was more than conventional grief. It meant bereavement of his nearest and dearest. When Elijah had spread his own cloak over Elisha, it had been a highly creative and expressive gesture. God had merely told him to anoint Elisha 'to succeed you as prophet'. Elijah chose to elaborate this into an adoption ceremony: let me provide for you; wear my very clothes. Covering with a cloak was also a sign of betrothal (Ruth 3:4,7,9; Ezekiel 16:8), a pledge of intimate sharing. Elisha understood the invitation to become not just a disciple or business associate, but the son Elijah had never had; he kissed father and mother good-bye.

Ten years later Elisha says good-bye again. The emotion of the scene shows the warmth of affection between the two. Elijah wants to spare his son the pain of conscious separation; Elisha prefers not to talk about it. As the hour approaches, Elijah can avoid the subject no longer, offering whatever blessing and favour Elisha wants. Elisha asks for the first-born son's inheritance (see Good News Bible's footnote to verse 9). This was not an inheritance of money or property – Elijah had none to give – but of his spiritual character and power.

Elijah acknowledges his right as son to have it. And as Elijah is swept to heaven, Elisha can only cry in his loss, 'My father, my father! You are gone!'

Elijah's successor
Elijah had known since Sinai that this was God's plan. It was a wholly new development; no previous prophet had been allowed to name or appoint his successor. This was the radical new idea that gave meaning to the second half of Elijah's life and story. His ministry was not to be a 'one-off'. His failure to put Israel right need not be so final after all. He would have a son to succeed him and carry on the good work.

And now Elisha has reached the point of understanding this and wanting it. 'Let me receive the power that will make me your successor.' As we all should, in front of a spiritual responsibility, he knows he can't do it; he needs God's power. A difficult request for Elijah to grant! He feels for Yahweh's answer, and it comes, once again in cryptic riddle-form: 'you will receive the power if you see me taken away from you; you won't if you don't.' The surface meaning sounded simple enough: stick around, don't let me out of your sight. Little danger of that; there was no way he could shake Elisha off! The underlying meaning emerged in the event. The chariot and horses of fire were not for the purely physical eye to see; they were God's inner presence in the outer, recordable whirlwind. They were his escort for the home-coming of one of his most redoubtable soldiers, the 'mighty defender of Israel'. They were precisely the spiritual war-forces on which Elijah had called and relied as he had won battle after battle through prayer. Elisha suddenly sees the point and gets hold of it. This is still clearer in the Hebrew, where he shouts, not 'Mighty defender', but 'The chariots and horsemen of Israel!' It was probably the rallying war-cry of King Ahab's charioteers, but Elisha applies it to a larger, stronger regiment. Till now he had seen only the earthbound dimensions of Elijah: one man against Baal. Now his eyes open to the true, heavenly reality: it is Elijah *plus* God's army. Not only that; to complete the astonishing paradox of how God works on earth, Elisha is also discovering that Elijah *is* God's army. His breathless shout appears to grasp that Elijah fights both *with* the cavalry 'in the air' and *as* the cavalry on the ground. 'My father! The chariots and horsemen of Israel!'

So Elisha's cry is one of triumph as well as grief. He *has* seen the vision of Elijah going home; and really *seen* it to understand it. In awaking to the truth of the spiritual issues at stake, he has received the power he needs; he knows that God's Spirit and heaven's armies fight with him. So deeply did this insight burn into him that it marked the rest of his ministry, and made him Elijah's successor at the deepest level: in this respect he *was* Elijah continued. The central achievement of defeating Syria (2 Kings 6) was to rely on his prophetic gift of second sight. At the critical encounter he would pray for his own servant to see the spiritual dimension now so clear to him: 'the hillside covered with horses and chariots of fire, all round Elisha' (verse 17). In all work we do for God, especially where his will runs into resistance and opposition, we too need to act on this knowledge that 'the Spirit who is in you is more powerful than the spirit in those who belong to the world' (1 John 4:4).

As the vision faded, Elisha became aware of something at his feet. It was Elijah's cloak. God could not have given him a more perfect token at this moment of taking up new responsibility. The one piece of earthly property that 'was' Elijah – his trade mark. And at the same time the family heirloom and badge of office that he had already promised to pass on to Elisha. As he handled the strong, rough clough, Elisha remembered his call at Abel Meholah, realized afresh that God would equip him, and resolved to live up to the example Elijah had set. He took the cloak in his hand and struck the water. As we take up any new task or duty that God has led us to, we can move forward boldly in this same confidence that he comes with us. Our predecessor may have been taken away, but God does not leave us. He may use a personal memento or keepsake – a text card, a bookmark, even a piece of clothing – to remind us that he is here.

Elijah's colleague
The talk of Elisha as pupil, son, successor must not obscure the fact that in some ways he was very different from Elijah. Their background, characters and gifts complemented each other to make them a first-rate partnership.

Elisha's call-scene in 1 Kings 19 shows how well God had shaped him for his future ministry, first as Elijah's helper and then alone. Elijah was poor, Elisha was wealthy; his father owned an estate with twelve teams of oxen. But Elisha was no idle slouch; he worked with the hired hands. As they worked together, he brought up the rear, supervising the job and the men. Elijah was a solitary, Elisha was sociable; he had a secure relationship with his parents and their extended family of retainers, for whom he threw a farewell party.

None of this was particularly useful for serving Elijah alone in some mountain retreat. It was, however, invaluable for what I suspect they were really doing, running a chain of prophetic training colleges. That is certainly what Elisha was doing a short while after Elijah's departure. He was in charge of a group of prophets at Gilgal, where he taught them (2 Kings 4:38; 6:1). The one recorded incident of Elijah and Elisha at work together shows them not exclusively wrapped up in their own company, but in relation with two groups of prophets. Indeed, it may well be three groups, as they set off from Gilgal, where Elisha's pupils could already have been living. Gilgal was later Elisha's home, and the clear inference of 2 Kings 2:1 is that it already was. It would certainly have been a nearer base than Carmel from which to launch Elijah's pre-emptive strike on Ahaziah's messengers in the previous chapter.

The purpose of the zigzagging tour in chapter 2 seems to be to pay a farewell visit to these groups of prophets. Good News Bible makes it sound like a series of extraordinary coincidences that Elisha happens to keep bumping into 'a group of prophets who lived there'. The Hebrew is more accurately translated in other versions, 'The company of prophets at Bethel and Jericho'. The whole point of the roundabout route from Gilgal to the Jordan was to meet them.

What strikes us immediately is that they talk to Elisha. He is the more approachable of the two.

To them Elijah is 'your master', more remote. If, as the second half of this chapter tries to demonstrate, these prophetic groups were Elijah's inspiration and creation, he could never have done it without Elisha. He was the visionary ideas man; he needed the human touch of Elisha the 'people person' to make it happen and work. There are tremendous strengths in working in a team. There are the natural advantages of support, encouragement, checks and balances, of two or more brains being better than one. In addition, Christians working together achieve more of God's will and represent more of his character than any single person could. Not many of us will find the son, the successor and the colleague in our lives all rolled together in the same person. But it is worth praying that God will give us such well matched companions as Elisha was, for the benefit that they bring.

We come again to Elisha's obituary of Elijah as '*Mighty* defender of Israel!' Elijah has been a better defence of Israel than the strong conventional army Ahab built up. Elisha is talking of a friend he has known intimately for at least ten years. His description 'Mighty defender' cannot simply be referring back to Carmel when Elijah indeed defended Israel against Jezebel's religion, but when Elisha probably hadn't even met him. It could to some extent refer to the later death sentences on Ahab's family, though these scotched attacks on Israel's faith that came from inside as much as outside. The epitaph would be far more apt if at the time when he was called 'upstairs', Elijah had just carried through a strategic programme designed to ensure the survival and spread of Yahweh's word through the land.

A group of prophets

We tend to think of prophets as lonely, individual geniuses – one against the multitude. Jeremiah, Jonah, Hosea spring to mind; and, of course, most influential of all, Elijah himself. Much more shadowy in the Old Testament are the teams of prophets working together. Yet they have just as long a pedigree.

They first appear with Saul (1 Samuel 10), a procession of prophets playing, dancing and shouting down the hill. Their enthusiasm is infectious and soon has Saul joining in too. Hence the proverbial saying, 'Has even Saul become a prophet?'; or in the more familiar English translation, 'Is Saul also among the prophets?' The kind of prophesying he and the band got up to was distinctly more ecstatic than coherent. This has led many to assume that the prophets we know by name (such as, in their generation, Samuel) would disapprove of their antics. So it comes as a shock, at their next appearance (1 Samuel 19:20), to find Samuel presiding over them. They seem to have been 'on the staff' at centres of worship, helping to lead the music and dance, and bringing a 'word from Yahweh' when someone consulted him. It was possible for their institutional appointment to work together with the more detached, critical stance of prophets who claimed Yahweh's appointment alone.

They evidently still existed in Ahab's reign, when Jezebel began her crusade to liquidate them and replace them with Baal prophets (1 Kings 18:4,13). There must have been large numbers of them, if

Obadiah could hide 100 without Jezebel noticing; her substitute corps was 850 strong. To all appearances she succeeded in stamping the Yahweh prophets out (verse 22). Barring the elusive Elijah, she had gagged the voice of God.

Almost the next time we see them they are in full flower under the cultivation of Elisha. The early chapters of 2 Kings give us the clearest picture of them in the Old Testament. They were under instruction (4:38) and mostly young (9:1). Their numbers were growing, so they needed extra accommodation (6:1–2). They lived in a flexible community: many of them lived (6:2) and ate together (4:38–44); but there was a separate house for Elisha (5:9). Not all the members were celibate youths; some lived in their own houses with wife and children (4:1–3). Modern Gilgal and Mehola may not be on exactly the sites of Elisha's two homes; but it is affecting that both today are 'moshavs', farming villages organized on a loosely communal structure, so retaining something of Elisha's imprint. His communities shared his independence of the court; they were deeply involved in politics, helping to fight wars (chapters 3,6,7), advising and anointing kings (9:1–10), but could show contempt for the king of Israel when merited (3:14). Later disciples of prophets wrote a record of their masters' messages; we may well owe our knowledge of Elijah's and Elisha's lives to these prophetic circles around Elisha.

There is no hint that Elisha was the creative, visionary mind behind all this initiative. It is significant that when we first see him at the prophetic colleges, it is *with Elijah* (2:1–5). And, for all their reserve, the students treat Elijah as their leader; it is only when they see that the power of Elijah is on Elisha that they bow and submit to him (2:15). Indeed the opening phase of chapter 2 reads like a tour of inspection of the colleges by the Principal, accompanied by the Pastoral Tutor.

At the time of Carmel the prophetic communities were virtually dead. They had been driven underground, with a maximum of 100 prophets left, cowering in two caves. By the end of Elijah's life, there are definitely two, probably three thriving colleges, with a total roll of at least 200. (The 50 novices from Jericho were not its full complement, 2:7.) There may have been other colleges as well; Elisha's visits to Carmel (2:25; 4:25) might indicate another foundation in Elijah's honour. It is hard not to trace Elijah's mind and hand in this sudden turnaround.

What seems to have happened is that Elijah remembered what Obadiah said about the 100, and reflected on it. He was still more impressed with God's closing words to him on Sinai: 'Yet I will leave seven thousand alive in Israel – all those who are loyal to me and have not bowed to Baal' (1 Kings 19:18). The tenses are more important than we stopped to notice in chapter four: 'the 7,000 *are already* loyal and true, I *will* protect them from judgment, in order to give hope for the future.' In this declaration of God's plan, Elijah heard his own recommissioning. A vital part of his re-education was to be the first teacher of the doctrine of the 'righteous remnant'. He learnt that even if there is no mass repentance; even if the majority continue to ignore Yahweh, God's plans are not defeated. He works through the small, faithful minority to take his kingdom forward. This truth is still an immense encouragement to small churches, small Christian Unions, even lone Christians today. The first to understand it was Elijah; and the first embodiment of it was the prophetic colleges he re-established.

With Elisha's help, perhaps Obadiah's too, he must have convened those that were left of the 100, and other suitable candidates from the 7,000. Whether he personally selected them, using his 'gown' in a homespun matriculation ceremony as he had with Elisha, or whether others simply turned up and volunteered, we have no idea. His motivation, though, was clear: to teach them all he knew, so as to re-activate the voice of Yahweh through law and prophecy for the future generations. He seems to have taught them well; three of their four speeches recorded in 2 Kings 2 mention Yahweh by name, and all four view life as under the control of his active Spirit. Elijah's genius was to revive an old institution – the prophetic community – and give it new, improved life and impetus.

Two other interesting facts may point back to Elijah's presiding genius. Before his time the prophetic groups were called 'bands'; the English word exactly combines the 1 Samuel 10 Hebrew word's double-flavour of a linked string or cord and a company of people gathered for a common purpose. When we meet them with Elijah in 2 Kings they have a new name, completely lost in Good News Bible's 'group'. They are called, literally, the 'sons of the prophets'. The name speaks, at the very least, of a shared family identity, of loyalty to their teachers and a sense of having something to preserve and pass on from one generation to the next. It may imply more about Elijah's feeling for them and theirs for him. Elisha was the 'firstborn son of the prophet'; but these others were also sons God had given him in the life he was learning to rebuild, a life of sharing. 'My father' may have been a customary way of addressing him. This would make Elijah the first abbot (derived from 'abba', daddy) of a monastic community. His Cherith and Zarephath training in simple lifestyle and community living came into play. It left its mark on the generation of prophets he schooled. The name 'sons of the prophets' was still in use for the prophetic schools or guilds some 90 years later when Amos came to prophesy in Israel. Good News Bible interprets Amos 7:14 as 'I am not the kind of prophet who prophesies for pay' (*i.e.* one of the professional, 'staff' prophets); his actual words were, 'I was neither a prophet nor one of the sons of the prophets'. In their different ways Bible and theological colleges, missionary seminaries, religious communities and modern experiments in extended family living or communities based on God's teaching have followed aspects of this tradition.

Elijah's influence may have lingered in another rather touching way. About 250 years later still, Zechariah prophesied to the exiles who had returned to the southern kingdom. He referred to prophets having a standard uniform of 'a coarse garment' (13:4). It is the same word as Elijah's famous 'cloak'. Who knows, perhaps those first sons of the prophet adopted his distinctive habit as a mark of respect, and set a trend for centuries to follow. Certainly Elisha berates his servant for accepting 'fine clothes' into the community (2 Kings 5:22–26).

At all events, whether or not I am right in crediting Elijah for it, prophecy revived in his lifetime. When Ahab was at war with Syria, after Carmel but before Naboth, he heard the unaccustomed sound of prophets other than Elijah addressing him in the name of Yahweh (1 Kings 20:13–22; 28; 35–43). None is named, but the impression given is of three different prophets; one of them comes from 'the sons of the prophets'. Where did they come from? Ultimately, from Yahweh. But the temptation to see them as Elijah's pupils is hard to resist.

Three years after Naboth's vineyard, Ahab died, fighting Syria again. He entered an alliance with Jehoshaphat, king of Judah, who said as every king of God's people should, 'first let's consult Yahweh' (1 Kings 22:5). Lo and behold, Ahab summons 400 court prophets. He has replaced Jezebel's Baal prophets with a sizeable contingent of Yahweh prophets. Unfortunately, in Elijah's view, they were not genuine; they were still under Jezebel's influence. Elisha later dismissed them to Ahab's son as 'those prophets that your father and mother consulted' (2 Kings 3:13). Jehoshaphat smells a rat too, because he instantly asks, 'Isn't there another prophet, through whom we can consult Yahweh?' (1 Kings 22:7). And there is; right inside Ahab's court – Micaiah son of Imlah. Ahab's reaction is true to form: 'I hate him, because he never prophesies anything good for me; it's always something bad' (verse 8). But he puts up with him.

When Micaiah steps forward, we hear the tones of true prophecy. 'I can see the army of Israel scattered over the hills like sheep without a shepherd. And Yahweh said, "These men have no leader; let them go home in peace." ... I saw Yahweh sitting on his throne in heaven, with all his angels standing beside him . . .' (1 Kings 22:17, 19). It is utterly individual, quite unlike the style of Elijah or Elisha. True prophets do not lose their own character when under the Holy Spirit's influence. And yet it is the same insight into heaven's view of the battlefield that Elijah and Elisha had; it is the same awareness of being a servant in God's presence in the court of heaven as Elijah displayed when he accosted Ahab twelve years before: 'In the name of Yahweh, whom I serve . . .'. Again it is sorely tempting to wonder whether Micaiah was a graduate of the Elijah-Elisha training scheme.

One way and another, Israel's ideological climate had improved out of recognition since that daring opening raid on Ahab's palace. The drought had halted the slide; Carmel had saved the true faith from going under; Gilgal and the other colleges had revived it. As Elijah stood on the river bank and looked at Elisha and the 50 prophets behind him, he knew that Yahweh's word would win through. His promise of the 7,000 was secure. This is reassurance for all who serve the God of Elijah and live on his word today. Elijah himself was no longer needed here; the time had come for the Lord to take him up.

For further reflection

1. In any responsibilities you have taken on as part of Jesus' church, who do you look on as (a) your 'Elijah', the person supervising and training you;

(b) your 'group' of colleagues and fellow-learners;
(c) your 'Elisha', the person who assists and will perhaps replace you? How could you strengthen the relationship with each?

2. Who do you see as today's successors of the groups of prophets? How do you think God wants to ensure that his word is widely heard in your country?

3. During Elijah's life, God's 'church' (his true followers) revived – perhaps largely through Elijah's vision and initiative. How would you like to see God's church grow and improve over the next 15 years? How do you think God might make use of you to help fulfil that vision?

Chapter seven

The man who never died

The time came for the LORD to take Elijah up to heaven in a whirlwind. Elijah and Elisha . . . kept talking as they walked on; then suddenly a chariot of fire pulled by horses of fire came between them, and Elijah was taken up to heaven by a whirlwind. Elisha saw it and cried out to Elijah, 'My father, my father! Mighty defender of Israel! You are gone!' And he never saw Elijah again.

In grief, Elisha tore his cloak in two. Then he picked up Elijah's cloak that had fallen from him, and went back and stood on the bank of the Jordan. He struck the water with Elijah's cloak, and said, 'Where is the LORD, the God of Elijah?' Then he struck the water again, and it divided, and he walked over to the other side. The fifty prophets from Jericho saw him and said, 'The power of Elijah is on Elisha!' They went to meet him, bowed down before him, and said, 'There are fifty of us here, all strong men. Let us go and look for your master. Maybe the spirit of the LORD has carried him away and left him on some mountain or in some valley.'

'No, you must not go,' Elisha answered.

But they insisted until he gave in and let them go.

The stable-lad burst into the transport office, clutching the memo he'd just received.

'What's all this about needing one of our chariots to pick someone up down there? We're the war department, not a taxi service.'

The porter on duty put down his newspaper. 'Dunno,' he said. 'I'll ring through to Deaths.'

As he waited, the stable-lad hummed the new spiritual they were learning in choir practice. 'Swing low, sweet chariot, Coming for to carry me home. . . .'.

'Dunno about the "sweet", mate,' said the porter, putting the receiver down. 'It's a *fiery* chariot.'

'Wow!' The lad's eyes bulged in their sockets. 'You mean we're taking the Chief on a battle? Chariots and horsemen of Israel! Death to the enemy! . . .'

'Hang on, hang on,' grumbled the porter. 'It's not a war. It's a Special Delivery.'

The boy whistled and his eyes gleamed. 'You mean we're bringing a man straight up without dying? Like Enoch in – whenever it was, Genesis 5, I think. Who is it this time?'

'Whodyerthink?'

'Hey, not Elijah! Coo, he's quite a lad – you can't keep him down, can you? Wey-hey, and I'll be at the gate when he arrives. . . . Here, but if it's a *fiery*, won't he get burnt?'

'He's not coming *in* the chariot; that's just a special effect. Royal escort. They're bringing him up in a whirlwind. Good, that, innit? A tornado lift for a tornado man. Now clear out of here while I get on to Weather and check they're ready. . .'.

Elijah was taken up to heaven

Elijah's exit was even more dramatic than his entrance. He went to heaven without dying. The exhaustive search of the 50 strong young men didn't find him because he wasn't there any more.

He would have been amazed and humbled to realize that he had gone one up on Moses. Some people say that Moses too did not die in the normal way, and the idea spread in the time between Old and New Testaments. But Deuteronomy 34:5–7 contradicts it: Moses died, even though no-one knows the exact place of his burial. His obituary at the end of that chapter shows why Elijah would never expect to equal his stature: 'There has never been a prophet in Israel like Moses; Yahweh spoke with him face to face. No other prophet has ever done miracles and wonders like those that Yahweh sent Moses to perform against the king of Egypt, his officials, and the entire country. No other prophet has been able to do the great and terrifying things that Moses did in the sight of all Israel.'

Yet there are obvious likenesses between the two. If Moses was the king of prophets, Elijah was the Crown prince. He would not have called himself 'a second Moses' as later generations have, but he set himself to restore Moses' teaching in the land. In the process he stumbled on new truths in God's unfolding revelation – 'the soft whisper of a voice', the faithful 7,000; but he set himself up less as a 'reformer' than a 're-former', recalling Israel to the covenant and law that had established it. His picture of God was the same as Moses': a flaming fire. His notorious hold on the rain had been based on God's promise and warning to Moses. When in trouble he headed back to Moses' meeting-place with God on Sinai. Now that his time has come, he makes across the Jordan to the lonely spot where Moses died. And as Elisha has insisted on coming too, he leads him to where he will have to retrace the steps of Joshua – the new spiritual leader, crossing the Jordan on dry land, sharing his master's spirit, to reclaim the country for Yahweh.

The description of Elijah's transfer from earth to heaven is another of the author's breathtaking understatements. A mere 24 words; not even a complete sentence. Yet it is one of the most luminous moments in human biography. The 600 words devoted to it in the last chapter have not exhausted its meaning; we shall need another 1,000 words now. When God steps down to earth in the Old Testament, the sparks fly and you feel the blast. He leads fire and tempest in his trail. As Elijah himself had learnt, they are not themselves God; he is not confined to them, nor do they express his innermost heart. But they show where he is; and he uses them to save his servants. 'Yahweh Almighty will rescue you with violent thunderstorms and earthquakes. He will send tempests and raging fire' (Isaiah 29:6).

You use the clouds as your chariot
  and ride on the wings of the wind.
You use the winds as your messengers
  and flashes of lightning as your servants.
(Psalm 104:3–4)

He comes with the brightness of lightning;
  light flashes from his hand,
  there where his power is hidden.
(Habakkuk 3:4)

Elijah's whirlwind and chariot meant that God himself reached down to take him up (verse 1). And with unspeakable tenderness, probably also with gentle humour, he lays on a stunning spectacular to match Elijah's perception of him as the Lord of hosts.

It was the most unusual 'death' in history. Yet it bursts with instruction and comfort as we face our own death, or that of those we love.

1. 'The time came . . .'

A Christian's life is not at the mercy of chance or fate; it is under God's control. He has his time for our life and work on earth to finish. Until that time, he keeps us safe, we are immortal; once the time comes, there is no giving him the slip.

When things are going badly, however low we feel, we should not pray to die before our time, as Elijah did (1 Kings 19:4). It is a prayer God did not, and will not, answer. Still less should we try to take our own life. God will provide the help we need to endure the ordeal, as he did for Elijah.

And when things are going well, an early death

such as Elijah's, death in our prime, is not the tragedy it may seem from a purely human viewpoint. The sting of tragedy is its sense of waste. But there is no waste if God's time has come. His earthly purpose is complete. Those left behind feel terrible loss and grief, as Elisha did. But God's time to take Elijah *up* was also his time to take Elisha *on* to new growth, new challenges he would never have found under Elijah's shadow. God's timing *is* perfect, however much we may feel out of step with it at the time.

2. '. . . *for the Lord to take* . . .'
Death is seldom fully orchestrated like Elijah's; we do not see the chariots of fire. We only see the collapse of the earthbound corpse, whether sudden or long drawn-out. Death looks like the most lonely experience in life. Elijah's passing gives us the fuller view. God comes to him and scoops him into his arms. We do not normally see God do this, but he is equally active and protective in the death of all his people. On the point of martyrdom Stephen called out, 'I see heaven opened and the Son of Man standing at the right-hand side of God! . . . Lord Jesus, receive my spirit!' (Act 7:56,59). Jesus must have been standing to greet Stephen and help him in; for his normal position in heaven is sitting, enthroned (Hebrews 1:3). Jesus had earlier taught God's involvement in our death in a graphic parallel. 'Do not be afraid of those who kill the body but cannot kill the soul . . . not one sparrow falls to the ground without your Father's consent (the Greek is simply, and *much* more intimately, '*without your Father*'). . . . So do not be afraid;

you are worth much more than many sparrows!'
(Matthew 10:28–31).

In his negro preacher's style, James Weldon
Johnson pictures this truth most movingly in his
funeral sermon, 'Go down Death'.

Day before yesterday morning,
God was looking down from his great, high
    heaven,
Looking down on all his children,
And his eye fell on Sister Caroline,
Tossing on her bed of pain.
And God's big heart was touched with pity,
With the everlasting pity.

And God said: Go down, Death, go down,
Go down to Savannah, Georgia,
Down in Yamacraw,
And find Sister Caroline.
She's borne the burden and heat of the day,
She's laboured long in my vineyard,
And she's tired –
She's weary –
Go down, Death, and bring her to me.

While we were watching round her bed,
She turned her eyes and looked away,
She saw what we couldn't see;
She saw Old Death. She saw Old Death,
Coming like a falling star.
But Death didn't frighten Sister Caroline;
He looked to her like a welcome friend.
And she whispered to us: I'm going home,
And she smiled and closed her eyes.

And Death took her up like a baby,
And she lay in his icy arms,
But she didn't feel no chill.
And Death began to ride again –
Up beyond the evening star,
Out beyond the morning star,
Into the glittering light of glory,
On to the Great White Throne.
And there he laid Sister Caroline
On the loving breast of Jesus.

And Jesus took his own hand and wiped away
    her tears,
And he smoothed the furrows from her face,
And the angels sang a little song,
And Jesus rocked her in his arms,
And kept a-saying: Take your rest,
Take your rest, take your rest.

Weep not – weep not,
She is not dead;
She's resting in the bosom of Jesus.

When we die, it is the Lord taking us home.

3. *'. . . up to heaven'*
Elijah's life ended in a blaze of glory; he was lifted
up to his reward. Here was God's visible 'yes' to
his life of endeavour. It has the same upward
dynamic as Jesus' resurrection: 'God raised him
from death, setting him free from its power,
because it was impossible that death should hold
him prisoner' (Acts 2:24). What God has brought
to life, you cannot nail down.
Few Old Testament writers understood that this

was the destiny of all God's people. They thought Elijah a glorious exception, raised to God's home because of his outstanding value. Death for others, they feared, was *down*, to the grave or the pit, a shadowy half-life out of God's sight and mind. And that's how it feels today. We see the body wizened and shrunk, the coffin lowered into cemetery or crematorium. Instinct sides with the modern climate of thought which believes only what we can see. We feel that death is a dead end, a mockery. We fear it, we hate it, but we give in. It seems we have no choice.

Quite the reverse. Glorious transformation. Jesus has ended this power of death 'and through the gospel has revealed immortal life' as the inheritance of all his followers (2 Timothy 1:10). In that same letter, Paul takes the positive, upward, 'Elijah' view of his own death: 'As for me, the hour has come for me to be sacrificed; the time is here for me to leave this life. . . . And now there is waiting for me the prize of victory awarded for a righteous life, the prize which the Lord, the righteous Judge, will give me on that Day – and not only to me, but to all those who wait with love for him to appear.' (4:6,8). Death is the crown of life. It is not the end, but the start of better, truer, fuller life in heaven.

4. '. . . we will be gathered up. . .'
Elijah's non-death draws back the curtains on everyone else's death. We have seen through him the true nature of death for all who die before the world does. On top of that, his ascension, along with Jesus', provides the prototype for those still alive at the end of the world. 'Those who have died

believing in Christ will rise to life first; then we who are living at that time will be gathered up along with them in the clouds to meet the Lord in the air. And so we will always be with the Lord.' (1 Thessalonians 4:16–17). We shall also always be with Elijah; in a smaller way, he too blazed the trail.

*　　*　　*

'Remember the teachings of my servant Moses, the laws and commands which I gave him at Mount Sinai for all the people of Israel to obey. But before the great and terrible day of the LORD comes. I will send you the prophet Elijah. He will bring fathers and children together again; otherwise I would have to come and destroy your country.' (Malachi 4:4–6)

But the angel said to him, 'Don't be afraid, Zechariah! God has heard your prayer, and your wife Elizabeth will bear you a son. You are to name him John.

From his very birth he will be filled with the Holy Spirit, and he will bring back many of the people of Israel to the Lord their God. He will go ahead of the Lord, strong and mighty like the prophet Elijah. He will bring fathers and children together again; he will turn disobedient people back to the way of thinking of the righteous; he will get the Lord's people ready for him.' (Luke 1:13,15b–17)

At that time John the Baptist came to the desert of Judea and started preaching. 'Turn away from your sins,' he said, 'because the Kingdom of heaven is near!'

John's clothes were made of camel's hair; he wore a leather belt round his waist, and his food was locusts and wild honey. (Matthew 3:1–2, 4)

The Jewish authorities in Jerusalem sent some priests and Levites to John, to ask him, 'Who are you?'
John did not refuse to answer, but spoke out openly and clearly, saying:
'I am the Messiah.'
'Who are you, they asked. 'Are you Elijah?'
'No I am not, John answered. (John 1:19–21a)

Until the time of John all the prophets and the Law of Moses spoke about the Kingdom; and if you are willing to believe their message, John is Elijah, whose coming was predicted. (Matthew 11:13–14)

When Herod, the ruler of Galilee, heard about all the things that were happening, he was very confused, because some people were saying that John the Baptist had come back to life. Others were saying that Elijah had appeared, and still others that one of the prophets of long ago had came back to life. Herod said, 'I had John's head cut off; but who is this man I hear these things about?' And he kept trying to see Jesus.
One day when Jesus was praying alone, the disciples came to him. 'Who do the crowds say I am?' he asked them.
'Some say that you are John the Baptist,' they answered. 'Others say that you are Elijah, while others say that one of the prophets of long ago has come back to life.' (Luke 9:7–9,18–19)

Then the disciples asked Jesus, 'Why do the teachers

of the Law say that Elijah has to come first?'

'Elijah is indeed coming first,' answered Jesus, 'and he will get everything ready. But I tell you that Elijah has already come and people did not recognize him, but treated him just as they pleased. In the same way they will also ill-treat the Son of Man.'

Then the disciples understood that he was talking to them about John the Baptist. (Matthew 17:10–13.)

I will send you the prophet Elijah

Elijah never died. His name and his influence live on through the rest of the Bible. And God promised that there would be a 'Return of Superman' Elijah. He did so in the two last verses of the Old Testament. Elijah would come before the final day of reckoning, that great and terrible day of Yahweh. . . . You can imagine how national fervour got to work with that. Just as the legend that King Arthur will return to Britain at a time of national need has lived on and surfaces again in a crisis, so the Elijah expectation has thriven among the Jews with their long history of persecution. To this day the Passover celebration contains a spare cup for Elijah in case he comes; at one point in the meal the door is opened to see if he is standing outside. At some circumcision ceremonies a seat is left empty for Elijah. When he comes, he will herald the Messiah.

At the time of Jesus, the Jews longed for the Messiah to liberate them from Roman occupation, and Elijah fever was rife. Was John the Baptist Elijah? Was Jesus Elijah? Some taught that Elijah, having never died, had been wandering the earth ever since, waiting for the moment to show himself. That explains the different interpretations of Jesus given to Herod: 'Some say he's John the Baptist *come back to life*, some that he's one of the prophets of long ago *come back to life*; others say that Elijah *has appeared*' (Luke 9:7–8).

The angel Gabriel told Zechariah that his son John would fulfil Malachi's prophecy: 'He will go ahead of the Lord, strong and mighty like the prophet Elijah' (Luke 1:17). John himself appears to put the Elijah name-badge on by dressing in the celebrated camel-hair cloak (Matthew 3:4 – though, as we have seen, this could be no more than the standard uniform of any prophet). Jesus twice identified John as the Elijah whose coming was predicted (Matthew 11:14; 17:11–13). Yet when the Jewish authorities asked John outright, 'Are you Elijah?', he answered 'No, I am not' (John 1:21). Why should he do this?

They were expecting Elijah himself to return or reappear. It is this literal 'reincarnation' that John denies. When John appeared as the last forerunner of Jesus he was not inhabited in some spiritualist sense by his greatest predecessor; he simply resumed Elijah's ministry. He took up the same task.

Elihah's mission had been to bring the people back to God (1 Kings 18:37). So was John's (Luke 1:16). This seems a more satisfactory understanding of the way Malachi describes Elijah-John's mission than Good News Bible's vision of family reunions healing the generation gap: 'He will bring fathers and children together again.' His actual words are, 'He will turn the heart of the fathers to the children, and the heart of the children to their fathers.' They follow directly the instruction, 'Remember the teachings of my servant Moses, the laws and commands which I gave him at Mount Sinai for all the people of Israel to obey' (4:4). The 'fathers' in his prophecy are the forefathers in the faith, Moses and all others who had been true to their calling. John's mission is to reunite his generation of the children of Israel with their ancestors in obeying the law of Moses. Gabriel echoes this prophecy in his announcement to John's father (Luke 1:17); he goes on at once to explain what it means, 'he will turn disobedient people back to the way of thinking of the righteous'.

John's *mission* is a re-run of Elijah's (in its purpose, not its detail). It therefore needs to be lived out in the same *spirit* as Elijah. John lives and dresses simply, but these are the externals. He is 'strong and mighty, like the prophet Elijah' (Luke 1:17); or, more literally, he works 'in the spirit and power of Elijah'. Just as Elisha received God's power to carry on Elijah's ministry, so did John. 'From his very birth he will be filled with the Holy Spirit' (verse 15).

Mission and spirit make Elijah 'speak again'; so the *message* is the same too. The first Elijah's was, 'Turn back to Yahweh from Baal, or the curse of drought will remain.' The 'second' Elijah would say, 'Turn back to the way of your fathers; otherwise God will come and destroy your country' (Malachi 4:6). John said, 'Turn away from your sins, because the kingdom of heaven is near! The axe is ready to cut down the trees at the roots;

every tree that does not bear good fruit will be cut down and thrown in the fire' (Matthew 3:2,10).

The message takes on added urgency and finality from its *aim*, because it is laying down the carpet for Jesus to walk on. 'He will go ahead of the Lord . . . he will get the Lord's people ready for him' (Luke 1:17). 'Elijah is indeed coming first,' said Jesus, 'and he will get everything ready' (Matthew 17:11).

This projects back on to Elijah's errand, and forward on to ours. John's charge was to get things ready for Jesus. But so, on a different time-scale, was Elijah's. And so, in a slightly different way again, is ours. This preparatory groundwork demanded that Elijah and John preach God's judgment: 'Turn – or else!' This is the starting-point for our message too. People cannot see what is so good about the Good News, until they have first heard and understood the bad news about the sins they must turn from.

We shrink from this because people don't like it. They claim to admire Jesus as teacher and example; unless his Spirit moves them, they do not want him as deliverer from their sins. This is why they ask for God's love without his law, or the New Testament without the Old; but you cannot have the one without the other. You cannot have the message of Jesus without the message of John or Elijah; eternal life starts with repentance.

Equally you cannot pass on the messsge of Jesus, or John and Elijah, without incurring their unpopularity. 'I tell you that Elijah has already come and people . . . treated him just as they pleased' (Matthew 17:12). John lost his head for accusing the king of breaking God's law; if Jezebel had had her way, Elijah would have lost his. 'In the same way they will also ill-treat the Son of Man.' In the same sort of way they may treat us. We had better be ready. Jesus said, 'Whoever does not take up his cross and follow in my steps is not fit to be my disciple' (Matthew 10:38).

*   *   *

About a week after he had said these things, Jesus took Peter, John and James with him and went up a hill to pray. While he was praying, his face changed its appearance, and his clothes became dazzling white. Suddenly two men were there talking with him. They were Moses and Elijah, who appeared in heavenly glory and talked with Jesus about the way in which he would soon fulfil God's purpose by dying in Jerusalem. Peter and his companions were sound asleep, but they woke up and saw Jesus' glory and the two men who were standing with him. As the men were leaving Jesus, Peter said to him, 'Master, how good it is that we are here! We will make three tents, one for you, one for Moses, and one for Elijah.' (He did not really know what he was saying.)

While he was still speaking, a cloud appeared and covered them with its shadow; and the disciples were afraid as the cloud came over them. A voice said from the cloud, 'This is my Son, whom I have chosen – listen to him!' When the voice stopped, there was Jesus all alone. (Luke 9:28–36a)

Elijah appeared in heavenly glory

Elijah was not literally John the Baptist. Yet he *did* reappear on earth before the great and terrible day of the Lord. It was once again on a mountain-top, the Mount of Transfiguration where earth and heaven met. Peter and his companions saw him in company with Moses and Jesus. Why these three? Moses was Elijah's great hero and inspiration from the past, and Jesus – though he had not known it at the time – was the great Future his efforts had helped to form. But why was he there with Moses and Jesus? Why not more 'up front' leaders in God's kingdom, such as Abraham or Joshua or David?

One key is that Moses, Elijah, Jesus are the three pioneers around whom the vast majority of Bible miracles cluster. Joshua, Elisha, the apostles continue their work; but the three on show at the transfiguration were the spearheads of God's new and unexpected initiatives at times when his plan seemed lost beyond retrieval and his followers had almost fizzled out in the dark. They were the three heralds of major advances or shifts of policy in God's dealings with his people. Jesus met his great forerunners.

They were also his *foretellers*. One of Jesus' first disciples said, 'We have found the one whom Moses wrote about in the book of the Law and whom the prophets also wrote about' (John 1:45). The Law and the Prophets were the two great streams of God's revelation pointing to the Messiah. Moses had no rival or partner as law-giver; but should Elijah really represent the prophets? He had no great book of oracles like Isaiah. He did not minister from youth to old age in the public eye like Jeremiah. He was aware of failure. He was not the first prophet; Moses himself and Samuel were leaders of massive stature who brought God's word to the people. Yet the Jews persisted in valuing Elijah as greatest of the prophets. Why?

The answer must lie in a blend of three things: the cosmic powers he seems to unleash – stopping the sky, raising the dead, calling down fire; the divine dimension to his short ministry – appearing from nowhere, praying heaven open, bypassing death, ushering in the day of judgment; and his herculean achievements – driving out a corrupt dynasty, halting the spread of Baal worship, securing the prophetic channel for God's voice to be heard as Israelite-Judaean history stumbled its way towards its climax in the Christ. It is all most beautifully expressed in a poem in the Apochrypha.

> How glorious you were, Elijah, in your miracles!
> Who else can boast such deeds?
> . . . Happy are those who saw you
> and were honoured with your love!
>
> (Ecclesiasticus 48:4,11)

The poem, which comes in a sequence of 'Heroes of Israel's past', is printed in full at the end of this book.

'Happy were those who saw him' – including Jesus. It was the crown of Jesus' perfect life on earth to walk into heaven, and see Elijah and Moses waiting to greet him. Jesus alone of all humanity had deserved to sidestep death and ride the winds home in this way. At the transfiguration he entered heaven in his glory and had every right to stay there. We watch transfixed: will he stay there, or will he step back on to earth? If he stays, of course, we shall never see him again.

Through the disciples' ears, we hear him talking with Elijah and Moses. What would we expect it to be about? Miracles, victories, successes, disappointments, glory, heaven. . . ? No. It's about one more thing Jesus must do to make God's purpose complete. Jesus' ultimate achievement is to go back down to die in Jerusalem. He will give up the heavenly glory to endure the pains of hell for everyone. Only so can the demands of Moses and the law, and the dreams of Elijah and the prophets, be fulfilled. Only so can we receive the right to enter heaven ourselves.

We echo Peter: 'Master, how good it is to be here on the Mount of Transfiguration with Elijah in heavenly glory! Let's read a biography about Elijah – reflect on it, learn from it.' And God takes the book on Elijah into the cloud. 'That's enough about Elijah,' he says. 'Elijah foreshadows Jesus, and points to him. Elijah was only a man, although a great one; Jesus is something more – he is God as well. Elijah was often full of my Holy Spirit as a human carrier – Jesus is the transmitter and dispenser of the Spirit. Rub Elijah hard enough and you come to Jesus underneath. *He* is my Son, my chosen – he is the one I want you to go on listening to.' So when the book stops and the cloud clears, we are left with Jesus all alone.

For further reflection

1. Do you know anyone approaching death? Is there any way you could help them to hold on to God's good news about death, as illustrated in the story of Elijah?

2. In what ways was Elijah like Moses, even a second Moses? In what ways were they different? How does this help you to reflect on what Elijah's life and ministry were all about? Why does the Book of Kings interrupt its record of royalty to devote six chapters to Elijah? Why does Elijah figure so prominently in the New Testament?

3. Why did Jesus remind people of Elijah? In what ways was Elijah like Jesus? How did he help prepare the way for Jesus? In what sense, if any, did he prophesy Jesus or foresee the New Testament?

In praise of a famous man

Then Elijah appeared, a prophet like fire,
whose word flamed like a torch.
He brought famine upon them,
and his zeal made their numbers small.
By the word of the Lord he shut up the sky
and three times called down fire.
How glorious you were, Elijah, in your miracles!
Who else can boast such deeds?
You raised a corpse from death
and from the grave, by the word of the
    Most High.
You sent kings and famous men
from their sick-beds down to their deaths.
You heard a denunciation at Sinai,
a sentence of doom at Horeb.
So you anointed kings for vengeance,
and prophets to succeed you.
You were taken up to heaven in a fiery
    whirlwind,
in a chariot drawn by horses of fire.
It is written that you are to come at the appointed
    time with warnings,
to allay the divine wrath before its final fury,

to reconcile father and son,
and to restore the tribes of Jacob.
Happy are those who saw you
and were honoured with your love!
    Ecclesiasticus 48:1–11 (New English Bible)

A prayer

Loving Father,

We thank you for the powerful witness of Elijah, who like a signpost shows us the way to go.

Not seeking to please people, nor fearing their anger and contempt, he cared only for your will and commandments and, in his burning zeal for your honour, sought the establishment of your kingdom.

Send down upon us the spirit of Elijah, that a fire may be set ablaze in us: 'Your kingdom come!' Fill us with ardour, that you may receive the love and honour that are your due. Grant that we may exert ourselves fully to this end and bring you our sacrifices, including the sacrifice of being opposed and deserted by others.

Amen.

Mother Basilea Schlink

For further study

There are as many different perceptions of Elijah
as there are people who have studied his story,
prayed over the challenge that it presents and tried
to follow his footprints. No one biography or
commentary can say it all. So I warmly recommend
these other publications which, each in a different
way, have excited me and humbled me in writing
this book. They will deepen your faith and wonder
at the God of Elijah.

F. B. Meyer, *Elijah and the secret of his power*
(re-issued by Lakeland, 1972).

Ronald S. Wallace, *A study guide to Elijah and
Elisha* (Africa Christian Press, 1957).

Harry Fernhout, *Of kings and prophets: A study
of the book of Kings* (Joy in learning Curriculum
Development and Training Centre, Toronto, 1979).

W. Phillip Keller, *Power! The challenge of Elijah*
(Word Books, 1980; UK edition: Bridge
Publishing, 1984).

Nora Rock, *Dothan the dreamer* (Scripture Union, 1985) – a children's book, but a most sympathetic portrait of Elijah through the eyes of his servant boy.

David Pawson, Bible teaching cassettes on Elijah, DP 30–36, available from Anchor Recordings, 72 The Street, Kennington, Ashford, Kent TN24 9HS.

Stand Back Superman, cassette pack including a presentation of the Elijah story in words and music, and Dick Lucas' sermon on 1 Kings 19:4, available from St Helen's Church, Great St Helen's, London EC3A 6AT.